The Brontës

Veins Running Fire

The incredible story of a literary family

DERICK BINGHAM

AMBASSADOR INTERNATIONAL
Greenville, South Carolina • Belfast, Northern Ireland

The Brontës - Veins Running Fire
© Copyright 2007 Derick Bingham

ISBN 978-1-84030-188-5

Ambassador Publications
a division of
Ambassador Productions Ltd.
Providence House
Ardenlee Street,
Belfast,
BT6 8QJ
Northern Ireland
www.ambassador-productions.com

Emerald House
427 Wade Hampton Blvd.
Greenville
SC 29609, USA
www.emeraldhouse.com

*'Why should it annoy you that I discovered your country?
Is Ireland then a Nazareth, a Galilee from which no prophet
or good thing can come?'*[1]

Charlotte Brontë to an anonymous correspondent
21 November 1863

to

Gordon, Dorothy, Alan and Mary

- the Brontës who lived next door -

LIST OF
Contents

8

Introduction
FROM DRUMBALLYRONEY TO THE AGES

COUNTY DOWN is in my blood. My spirit is edged by the changing face of Slieve Donard; now purple shaded, now forbiddingly dark, now showing glistening winks of Mourne granite in the sun as it breaks through yet another 'sunshine shower that never lasts half an hour.'

Drenched in many a million such showers the switchback drumlin hills of County Down, shaped like the back of a spoon by receding glaciers, have been ploughed and tilled for centuries by formidable people. Within the county is the Kingdom of Mourne where I lived for over 30 years. The time came, though, when I had to move on:

At thirty-three-and-a-half years of age I left behind
The Kingdom of Mourne where you can find
Nature spreading puffballs, ceps and shaggy ink-caps,
Where you can walk up Deer's Meadow and the Hare's Gap,
Where you'll find the Brandy Pad and Butter Mountain,
And drumlins by the thousand for the counting;
Where you'll see the Rowan Tree River and Slievemageoh,
Or Crocknafeola, but I had to go.[2]

I'm not the only one who for one reason or another 'had to go'. From this beautiful county at thirteen years of age Francis Crozier, who was born in Avonmore House on Church Square in Banbridge, joined the Royal Navy. He was to become the unsurpassed seaman of the Antarctic. Serving under Captain James Clark Ross on a four-year expedition to the ice they effected the greatest feat of navigation in the nineteenth century. The seaman from Banbridge sailed as Second-in-Command on Sir John Franklin's fateful North-West Passage expedition in which all one hundred and twenty-nine men perished. Captain Crozier took command after Franklin's death and led the courageous battle to survive in the Arctic wilderness. In the bitter life-or-death struggle, which lasted for years, Crozier, according to legend, was last to die – the last man standing.[3]

In the twentieth century, C S Lewis loved the county with a passion. In his autobiography he asks his reader to 'step a little way' from his father's house on the Circular Road in Belfast: 'Only two fields and across a lane and up to the top of the bank on the other side – and you will see, looking south with a little east in it, a different world. And having seen it, blame me if you can for being a romantic. For here is the thing itself, utterly irresistible, the way to the world's end, the land of longing, the breaking and blessing of hearts. You are looking across what may be called, in a certain sense, the plain of Down, and seeing beyond it the Mourne Mountains.'[4]

Within sight of those mountains in the same century a lad of fourteen started work on the family farm at Growell near Dromara. His mother's two stepsisters became the first women doctors in Ireland and he was to become one of the island's greatest engineers. He built his own aeroplane and made the first flights in Ireland, including one of three miles at Newcastle,

County Down on the 5 August 1910 watched by thousands of people, including my mother. But he did more. 'When the history of the twentieth century is written, Harry Ferguson's tractor system will be recognised as one of the greatest inventions amongst a galaxy of inventions such as aeroplanes, radio, TV, computers, and space exploration to mention but a few. It has enabled agriculture to greatly increase food production, and reduce the cost of food, without which many more of the ever-increasing world population could be faced with starvation.'[5]

In the same county, in the same century, Frank Pantridge was born in the town of Hillsborough and became the 'Father of Emergency Medicine' with his invention of the portable defibrillator. His work has saved untold numbers of lives as frontline ambulances across the earth are now fitted with his life-saving invention. Frank Pantridge served in the British army in the Second World War and was awarded the Military Cross during the fall of Singapore. He was captured by the Japanese and served as a slave labourer on the Burma Railway.

So it has been that from the hills and valleys of County Down that farmers, musicians, artists, engineers, writers, politicians, medics and entrepreneurs have risen to leave the world a better place.

In the world of spirituality St Patrick's boat was swept through the Strangford Lough tidal narrows in County Down in AD432 and Patrick is reputed to have preached his first sermon at Saul near the present county town of Downpatrick. A local chieftain gave him a barn for holding services.

In St Patrick's trail have come some truly outstanding County Down Christians who have touched the world with their witness. One moving story proves the point. The dying John Keats, arguably the greatest romantic poet in English literature, visited

County Down entering through the port of Donaghadee. Eventually, Keats, sadly suffered physical collapse through consumption. As he was dying in rooms taken at the bottom of the Spanish Steps in Rome he was nursed with great tenderness by his Christian friend, the artist Joseph Severn, who was later to become the British Consul in Rome.

On Christmas Eve 1820, the very sick Keats 'confessed something that had been troubling him for weeks, his intense spiritual yearning now that he was faced with possible death. "You know, Severn, I can't believe in your book the Bible. But I feel the horrible want of some faith – some hope – something to rest on." There was one book above all, ventured Keats, one book which might help him find some hope, some faith, give him something to rest on, the famous *Holy Dying* of Jeremy Taylor.'[6] Severn tracked the book down in Rome through Keat's doctor and every day, until he died on 23 February 1821, Severn read from its pages, affording Keats 'great comfort' and helping to settle his mind.[7] Severn always believed that John Keats came to faith before his death.[8]

Jeremy Taylor, sometimes known as 'The Shakespeare of Divines' became, in fact, Bishop of Down and Connor. He rebuilt Dromore Cathedral in County Down in 1661 and is buried there. He is but one outstanding example of Christians who have been born or lived in the county who have had enormous spiritual influence, under God, upon Christian witness.

Joseph Scriven who was born in Seapatrick, County Down in 1819 wrote the hymn, *What A Friend We Have In Jesus*. Today, for example, 23 million Japanese a year sing it in wedding ceremonies![9] That is 20% of the population of Japan. Interestingly, the hymn writer and composer Keith Getty who, with Stuart Townend, wrote one of the world's most popular hymns of the first part of the 21st century, *In Christ Alone*, comes from the City of Lisburn in County Down.

There have often been gifted schoolteachers across the centuries in County Down. The story is told about one who organised explorations of the Mourne Mountains during the summer holidays. He led the older boys from his school and some of their elder brothers on the explorations. On one trip the party got separated on Slieve Donard and, in a thick mist, lost their way. Much alarm was caused to their families when they did not return home at the appointed time. It was several days before they all reached home, full of romantic stories of hairbreadth escapes and thrilling adventures. The story is also told of this same teacher leading skating expeditions. Once when they were in the middle of a frozen lough the ice broke with a mighty crack, but the schoolteacher kept his cool and steered his whole party safely to the shore.[10]

Who was the hero behind these stories? He was born, apparently, in a two-roomed, whitewashed, thatched peasant cabin at Emdale in the Parish of Drumballyroney in County Down on St Patrick's Day 1777.[11] His name was variously spelt Patrick Prunty, Brunty, and Bruntee, until he himself decided to settle with Brontë when he became a student at Cambridge University. He too 'had to go' from County Down. Through his fascinating life and spiritual journey English literature was to be influenced forever. His veins were to run with passionate Christian zeal and compassion which was in turn to touch the lives and writing of his three daughters – Emily, Charlotte and Anne – when they appeared on the pages of literary history.

Much has been written about the remarkable Brontë family. Why, then, you may ask would I want to write about it? That my wife's late Uncle Gordon was Patrick's great-grand-nephew certainly sparked a deep interest in his fascinating family background. That he and his family were my neighbours in Belfast constantly reminded me of the heritage that was very close to my everyday life. That his widow Dorothy, who taught my children in Primary School, still lives next door, keeps that link in my consciousness with the family whose Irish roots have become part of English literature's legacy. That my wife shared a flat with her uncle's niece, née Anne Brontë, when at college, a niece who looks remarkably like Richmond's portrait of Charlotte Brontë, also deeply intrigued me.

In a sense, though, I have been stung into writing this book. Millions of people, including me, have been gripped by the BBCs 2006 production of *Jane Eyre,* now reckoned to be one of the greatest novels ever written. Yet Toby Stephens, who brilliantly played Rochester in the BBC production, stated that 'where modern readers sometimes dislike Jane's moralising digressions as the novel's narrator, this new adaptation "has relieved her of that."'[12] I was aghast.

Charlotte Brontë had a worldview that was decidedly Christian. A worldview is, of course, a set of assumptions about the basic make-up of the world. Christianity was her starting point. The worldview of any writer shapes what they write and Charlotte was no exception. 'In her pre-Darwinian belief in the truth of Scripture,' wrote Lucasta Millar in her book, *The Brontë Myth*, 'Charlotte was anything but modern. As a child she declared that the Bible was the best book in the world, and it is the book to which she most often alludes in her adult fiction. The daughter of one clergyman and the future wife of another, she was not a free-thinker like the atheist Harriet Martineau or the agnostic George Eliot, and her beliefs about literary creativity or "genius" were bound up with her religious perspective of life.'[13]

Charlotte's worldview is clearly seen in her novel *Jane Eyre* when Jane faces the almost overwhelming emotional, sexual and spiritual tension between the Christian view of marriage and the freethinking Edward Rochester's view. At the very heart of this masterpiece of English literature is Christian morality. I believe *Jane Eyre* to be one of the most powerful pieces of literature ever written in defence of the sanctity of marriage. It is moralising at its greatest and most creative level. To moralise is to comment on issues of right and wrong. It is no bad thing. To read Anne Brontë's neglected but superb novel, *Agnes Grey*, and her ten-page discussion of divine and human love in the chapter entitled, The Cottagers, is to realise that Anne had close knowledge of the chief religious issues of her times. The worldly Rev Hatfield's lack of knowledge of the workings of divine and human love is powerfully exposed. The devout Rev Weston's exposition of the subject to the poor, anxious and infirm Nancy Brown is altogether more helpful and comforting.[14] The novel, as a whole, also poignantly highlights the inhuman and contemptuous attitude shown towards poor though educated women in the Victorian age whose only resource was to become a governess. The novel has deep resonance towards the teaching profession even in the 21st century.

Emily Brontë who is, arguably, the least moralising of the three Brontë novelists is not entirely devoid of it. The exploration of spirituality is decidedly Gothic in *Wuthering Heights* and violence and coarse language are prevalent, to say the least. Heathcliff, one of the most enduring of literary characters, raises all kinds of questions regarding upbringing, love, marriage, revenge and life after death. The narrator of the story, Nelly Dean, most certainly moralises. She condemns

Heathcliff's brutality and his 'selfish unchristian life' while still holding some compassion for him.

'If you would hear me without being angry,' Nelly challenges Heathcliff, when he refuses to repent of his injustices, 'I might offer you some advice that would make you happier.'

'What is that?' he asked. 'Give it.'

'You are aware, Mr Heathcliff,' I said, 'that from the time you were thirteen years old, you have lived a selfish, unchristian life; and probably hardly had a Bible in your hands, during all that period. You must have forgotten the contents of the book, and you may have space to search it now. Could it be hurtful to send for someone – some minister of any denomination, it does not matter which, to explain it, and show you how very far you have erred from its precepts, and how unfit you will be for its heaven, unless a change takes place before you die?'[15]

The portrayal of Joseph, the hypocritical Calvinist in *Wuthering Heights* (somewhat like Willie Fisher the hypocritical elder of Mauchline immortalised by Robert Burns in his poem *Holy Willie's Prayer*) is a downright condemnation of someone whose Christianity does not walk the talk. Who could ever forget Nelly's comments that Joseph 'was, and is yet, most likely the wearisomest self-righteous Pharisee that ever ransacked a Bible to rake the promises to himself, and fling curses on his neighbours?'[16] God knows such Pharisees are still with us in today's world. Moralising? Unforgettable moralising, I'd say.

'Your cold blood cannot be worked into a fever – your veins are full of ice-water – but mine are boiling, and the sight of such chillness makes them dance,' Catherine tells Heathcliff.[17] The phrase could be attributed to the Brontë family in general. Their veins not only boiled with passion of one kind and another; they, to borrow a phrase from *Jane Eyre,* ran fire.[18]

Patrick's veins ran with evangelical fire. Charlotte's veins ran with sexual and feminist fire. Anne's veins ran with every bit as much feminist fire as Charlotte's mixed with the flames of doubt and deep devotion. Matthew Arnold wrote in his poem, *Haworth Churchyard*, that Emily was Byronic in the 'might, passion, vehemence, grief and daring' of her writing. He called Byron that 'world-famed Son of Fire'.[19] So it was that Emily's veins ran with the fire of nineteenth century Romanticism.[20] The much-maligned Branwell Brontë's veins ran with gifted poetic and artistic fire eventually fuelled, sadly, with alcohol and heroin addiction.

The story of the Brontës and their times runs with passion, immense talent, extraordinary powers of observation edged at all times by surrounding sickness and poverty. They lived their lives in a culture of Victorian death. In the end, the unimaginable fortitude that surfaces in a family facing sorrow upon sorrow, tragedy upon tragedy, is hugely inspiring.

Perhaps Charlotte caught this fortitude best when she wrote of her sisters in the 1850 edition of *Agnes Grey*. Of Emily, who died in December 1848 at thirty years of age, she wrote: 'Day by day, when I saw with what a front she met suffering, I looked on her with anguish of wonder and love. I have seen nothing like it; but, indeed, I have never seen her parallel in anything. Stronger than a man, simpler than a child, her nature stood alone.'

Of her sister, Anne, who died in May 1849 at twenty-nine years of age, Charlotte stated: 'I have said she was religious, and it was by leaning on these Christian doctrines in which she firmly believed that she found support through her most painful journey. I witnessed their efficacy in her latest hour and greatest trial, and must bear my testimony to the calm triumph with which they brought her through.'[21]

This book attempts to look at this extraordinary family particularly in the setting of their times. It aims to show how Patrick Brontë rose from the parish of Drumballyroney in Ireland to the heart of the reforming evangelical movement within the Anglican Church of the nineteenth century. It will show how he was personally sponsored by the great William Wilberforce through university. It will highlight his close association with the world famous Cambridge evangelical leader, the Rev Charles Simeon, and his circle. It will look at how the experience of being raised in an evangelical home affected the moral stance and themes of the novels written by his daughters. The book will also highlight the inspiring courage and tenacity of the awesomely gifted Brontë sisters to overcome incredible difficulties to write their way into the heart of world literature.

It was quite a journey from Drumballyroney to the ages but Patrick Brontë and his family made it, with flair.

Derick Bingham
Belfast
September 2007

PS The author wishes to sincerely thank Ms Dorothy Boyd, MIQPS for her most enthusiastic and patient help in typing this book for publication. She became, in the process, a distinct devotee of Anne Brontë.

ONE
Scorn of Ridicule

THE BEAUTIFUL hills of County Down have not always been solely bedecked with nature's benevolence; they have also been horrendously stained by human blood. Such a staining took place in 1798. Roman Catholics, Presbyterians and other non-conformists had for most of the eighteenth century been excluded from representation in the Irish Parliament. Only the land-owning Episcopalian class, known as the Ascendancy, were represented. It was all patently unfair.

There were two factors that fostered the deep desire for political reform. Ulster Presbyterians had migrated to colonial America in huge numbers between 1718 and 1775. Their relatives back at home greatly sympathised with the American War of Independence. They felt they were also subject to great injustice and they stood up for the cause of the American colonist revolt of 1775. The second factor was the French Revolution of 1789. So it was that many Roman Catholics, Presbyterians and other non-conformists across Ireland eventually joined the Society of United Irishmen that sought independence from British rule.

The British Government responded to the movement in a brutal anti-insurrection campaign, particularly in Ulster, by a roving campaign of disarmament. They did not flinch from using terror as a weapon. Some of the heaviest fighting in the United Irish Rebellion of 1798 took place in the County Down town of Ballynahinch. The battle began at 3.00am on 13 June and the rebels, though taking a terrible toll, pressed on with pike and bayonet pushing the military into Meeting House Street. A cavalry charge was ordered but it failed to dislodge the insurgents. A general retreat was then ordered from the town. The rebels mistook the bugles calling retreat for a signal that government reinforcements had arrived and both armies began to retreat simultaneously. Soon, though, the military learned the true situation and returned to the attack, eventually causing the rebels to retreat.

The cavalry was now ordered to pursue those rebels fleeing from the town. It was a fearful afternoon of bloodshed and atrocity, the worst of which has now passed deep into folklore.

In a marshy hollow at Ballycreen, about two miles from Ballynahinch, Betsy Gray, who we are told led the insurgents at Ballynahinch on a white horse, was taken by the Hillsborough Yeoman Cavalry. Her brother, George, and her fiancé, Willie Boal, went to her aid and were instantly shot down. A cavalryman struck off Betsy's gloved hand with his sabre and Thomas Nelson 'of the Parish of Annahilt aided by James Little of the same place' shot her through the head. Betsy Gray became known as Ulster's own Joan of Arc.[1] There has been a subsequent tug of war between Catholics and Protestants to claim her memory.

The nineteenth century poet, Mary Balfour, wrote of Betsy (calling her 'Bessie'):

The star of evening slowly rose,
Through shades of twilight gleaming,
It shone to witness Erin's woes,
Her children's life-blood streaming:
'Twas then, sweet star, thy pensive ray,
Fell on the cold unconscious clay,
That wraps the breast of Bessie Gray
In softened lustre beaming.[2]

One rebel, though, escaped capture as he fled the town and made his way deep into South Down and the Parish of Drumballyroney. His name was William Prunty.[3] William was the second son of Hugh and Eleanor. Hugh, though not wealthy, was a successful, hard working farmer and, apparently, he and Eleanor began their married life in the already mentioned two-roomed, whitewashed, peasant cabin at Emdale in the Parish of Drumballyroney. They later moved to larger premises in Lisnacreevy and Ballynaskeagh in the same parish.

As also already noted, their first son Patrick proved to be an exceptional individual for his or any time. He was allowed, it appears, to stay at school until he was sixteen and had possibly stayed on as a pupil teacher. He then established his own public school at sixteen, which he ran for five or six years.[4] There is indication that he taught the sons of the gentry in his school.[5]

In the momentous year that William Prunty sneaked home to Drumballyroney from the battle of Ballynahinch, mercifully escaping punishment, his brother Patrick made one of the most important decisions of his life. He decided to take up an appointment as tutor to the children of the Rev Thomas Tighe, vicar of Drumballyroney and rector of Drumgooland. Here was no mean man. He was to remain vicar for fifty-six years, was called 'the father of Irish evangelism' and built the parish schoolroom in 1778. The son of a Member of Parliament of Rosanna in County Wicklow and half-brother to two members of the Irish Parliament, Thomas Tighe was at the heart of the Ascendancy in the Ireland of his times. He was a Justice of the Peace and chaplain to the Earl of Glendore.   Schooled at Harrow, a graduate of St John's College, Cambridge and a Fellow of Peterhouse, Thomas Tighe was no rebel.[6]

When, at 21 years of age, Patrick Prunty accepted the position of tutor to Tighe's children, it is quite clear that Patrick was distancing himself from his brother William's political stance. When Patrick rose to prominence he was ever a staunch Unionist and roundly denounced rebellion. He always had a fear of it. It is felt that his political position was forged in the cauldron of the 1798 rebellion which had erupted around him.[7] Patrick was to be no friend of the writings of radical and revolutionary Tom Paine or of the French Revolution itself which brought the dawn of 'the golden age of atheism' that erupted into Western civilisation on 14 July 1789 when he was twelve years old.[8] He was never to acquiesce with Wordsworth's sentiment when he wrote that 'bliss was it in that dawn to be alive – but to be young was very Heaven!'[8]

Alister McGrath points out that 'the real atheism of this period is to be found in the writings of La Mettrie, Baron d'Holbach and Helvétius.   Whereas Voltaire and his Deist colleagues sought to rearrange existing understandings of the relation of the transcendent to everyday life, these more radical writers sought to eliminate the transcendent altogether.' He adds that 'whereas Isaac Newton (1674-1727) had argued that the regularity of planetary motions was evidence of divine design and governance of the universe, d'Holbach argued that they could not be accounted for on purely materialistic grounds. Belief in God is the product of a misguided human imagination, not the rigorous scientific application of the senses. The vigorous application of the scientific approach should therefore lead to atheism.' All this was to lead to 'the three great pillars of the golden age of atheism' – Ludwig Feuerbach, Karl Marx and Sigmund Freud. They helped create the mind-set of modern atheism.[9]

Patrick Prunty was to have a very different mind-set. As he grew up in Drumballyroney, another movement in Europe had gloriously taken hold and it is important in any biography dealing with Patrick and his family to understand its origins and worldwide influence. It was guided by a nation-changing incident on the evening of 24 May 1738 in London. 'I went unwillingly,' wrote John Wesley in his *Journal*, 'to a society in Aldersgate Street where one was reading Luther's *Preface to the Epistle to the Romans*. About a quarter before nine, while he was describing the change which God works in the heart through faith in Christ, I felt my heart strangely warmed. I felt I did trust in Christ, Christ alone, for salvation; and an assurance was given me that he had taken away my sins, even mine and saved me from the law of sin and death.'[10]

Later, Wesley told a friend called Samuel Broadburn when they were together in Yorkshire in 1781 that his Christian experience might be expressed in his brother Charles' hymn:

O Thou who camest from above
The pure, celestial fire to impart,
Kindle a flame of sacred love
On the mean altar of my heart.

There let it for Thy glory burn,
With inextinguishable blaze;
And, trembling, to its source return
In humble love and fervent praise.

Jesus, confirm my heart's desire
To work and speak and think for Thee;
Still let me guard the holy fire,
And still stir up thy gift in me.

Ready for all Thy perfect will,
My acts of faith and love repeat,
Till death Thine endless mercies seal,
And make the sacrifice complete.

The kindling in John Wesley's heart was to be felt around the earth, never mind speaking of his nation. It was a nation awash with a tidal epidemic of gin drinking and gambling. Sir George Trevelyan claimed 'society in those days was one vast casino.'[11] There was widespread indulgence in cruel and degrading sports. Violent crime soared. Prisons were over-crowded. Youth gangs clashed on the streets. Satanism was present. In one of his essays in the *Edinburgh Review*, Lord Jeffrey in retrospect complained that 'a greater mass of trash and rubbish never disgraced the press of any country than the novels that filled and supported circulating libraries.'[12]

As for the state of marriage, Lady Mary Montague declared that in society the 'state of matrimony is as much ridiculed by our young ladies as it used to be by young fellows; in short, both sexes have found the inconveniences of it, and the appellation of rake is as genteel in a woman as a man of quality.'[13] The theatre of the age was full of lewdness and the rank indecency of

Restoration drama. The first two Hanovarian monarchs were 'flagrantly dissolute' and the Prime Minister, Sir Horace Walpole (1722-1742), lived in 'undisguised adultery' with his mistress.[14]

As for the spiritual state of the nation, Daniel Defoe had declared 'no age, since the founding and forming of the Christian church in the world, was ever like it (in open and avowed atheism, blasphemies and heresies) to the age we now live in.'[15] As most preachers in the pulpits of the nation insipidly moralised, what the people needed most was a spiritual awakening and a saving.

Wesley was determined to let his nation know that there was a salvation to be experienced as he had experienced it. He believed in the importance of a reconnecting of head and heart through a living personal faith in Christ. This was a high tenet of Pietism, a movement coming out of the Lutheran Church on the mainland Europe of his day which had begun to lose the connection.[16]

Wesley rose for sixty years at 4.00am and preached at 5.00am. He preached at least twice and, sometimes, three or four times daily. He became a highly successful open air preacher facing mobs and stoning and huge persecution. He was forced to preach in the open air because many churches at the time would not have him. He always claimed to be an Anglican at heart. It is recorded that he travelled 4,500 English miles a year, mostly on horseback, and ultimately he founded the Methodist Church. Multitudes came to faith in Christ alone for salvation through his ministry.

The evangelical fire of Wesley's preaching also spread to the island of Ireland. In fact, John Wesley's forty-three year mission to Ireland resulted in the conversion of some 14,000 people not only to Methodism but, more importantly, to personal faith in Christ.[16]

He became a friend of the Tighe family at Rosanna and he stayed with them in June 1789 on his last visit to Ireland, eighteen months before his death. One month after his visit to Ireland the Bastille was stormed in Paris but Wesley had, by the grace of God, lit a fire that would ultimately help save his own country from revolution. Significantly, his very last letter was to William Wilberforce encouraging him in his drive to abolish the slave trade.

The evangelical and Wesleyan connections in the Tighe family were to play some of the most important of all influences on the life of Patrick Prunty. The Rev Thomas Tighe was a thorough-going evangelical and itinerant evangelical preachers were warmly welcomed at Drumballyroney rectory.[17] Professor Marianne Thormählen has pointed out that 'two of the most important influences on Patrick's life were Wesleyan Methodism and evangelicalism in the Church of England,' and, she states, 'it was his spell as tutor to Tighe's children which introduced him to that evangelical brand of Protestantism which shaped his future career.'[18]

Dr Juliet Barker, the outstanding authority on the Brontës and for six years curator and librarian of the Brontë Parsonage Museum in Haworth, sensitively and sympathetically gets to the very heart of the issue. She dismisses any suggestion that Patrick's journey to the Christian ministry within the Anglican Communion, which was deeply encouraged by the Rev Thomas Tighe, was driven by worldly ambition. There is no question that many a young man in the eighteenth century entered the Church to primarily better himself but Dr Barker wisely states that though Patrick's ambition cannot be doubted 'neither can his personal faith'. She argues that if he had primarily wanted to better himself, entering the Church under the aegis of the evangelicals was 'effectively curtailing his chances of future promotion, for evangelical clergyman were, as yet, only a small group within the Church and their progress met with considerable resistance from the all-powerful High Church party.'[19]

In truth, Patrick experienced a personal conversion to Christ and was an evangelical by conviction as his writings and activities clearly indicate. The cost of his actions regarding worldly ambition never weighed heavily with him.

While Patrick tutored the Tighe children at Drumballyroney, he felt the call of God to the Christian ministry within the Anglican Communion but he had a mountain to climb. That he conquered it was no light achievement. He first needed to enter university and for that he needed to be proficient in Latin and Greek. He could not have received this classical education in any local village school and it is thought that he got it from the Rev Tighe.

What thoughts, though, passed through the mind of the County Down farmer's son as he tutored the Tighe children over four years at Drumballyroney? Did he have self-doubt? What requests filled his prayers? What conversations did he have with his parents or with his brothers and sisters, William, Hugh, James, Welsh, Jane, Mary, Rose, Sarah and Alice?[20] What did they think of their brother's evangelical commitment and his desire to enter university at St John's College, Cambridge no less?

Famed for its evangelical connections, St John's College had been founded in 1511 by Lady Margaret Beaufort, mother of King Henry VII. In Patrick's day it had large funds available, more than any other Cambridge College, for poor but able students to get a university education. The fact that the Rev

Tighe had gone there, no doubt, naturally encouraged him to point Patrick in its direction.

So it was that Patrick Prunty left his family and the gentle rolling hills of South Down behind. Elizabeth Gaskell put it very succinctly when she wrote: 'He never could have shown his Celtic descent in the straight Greek lines and long oval of his face; but at five-and-twenty, fresh from the only life he had ever known, to present himself at the gates of St John's proved no little determination of will, and scorn of ridicule.'[21]

Two

A Desire of Usefulness

THE FRONT of what is known as the Great Gate of St John's College, Cambridge has seen a lot of students in its time. Completed in 1516 it contains a carving of the Coat of Arms of the foundress, Lady Margaret Beaufort. Above is a statue of St John the Evangelist, the writer and disciple of Jesus Christ. The heavy wooden gates used today date from 1665 and on 1 October 1802 they were open to register a new undergraduate from Drumballyroney in Ireland. The young Irishman was poor, but hopeful. Patrick Prunty had left Ireland with £7 in his pocket and, before that was spent, he received £5 from a distant friend. He had lived on this for some weeks before entering the college to register.[1]

History often swings on what seems to be tiny, insignificant incidents. Patrick gave his name to the registrar who, unaccustomed to a County Down accent, made a stab at trying to understand it. He entered the name 'Patrick Branty' in the admissions book.[2] Two days later when Patrick came back to take up residence in the college it is assumed that he found that the bursar had spelt his name incorrectly and challenged it. The entry was certainly altered in the College Residence Register from 'Branty' to 'Bronte'. It is again assumed that this was the moment when Patrick plucked the name 'Bronte' for his own possession.[3]

Why did Patrick choose the name Bronte, which was later to have the famous diaeresis added? Some reckon that he was imitating the title of Duke of Bronte which had been conferred on the great British naval hero, Horatio Nelson. Nelson had distinguished himself in the Mediterranean theatre of war against Napoleon Bonaparte and the King of the Two Sicilies had conferred the title on him. Bronte is the name of a village in Sicily. Whatever happened, the name of Bronte stuck and, unknown to Patrick at the time, it was to become a name forever associated with the history and genius of English literature. Forty years later, after the publication of *Jane Eyre*, it was rumoured about London that the Brontë's 'are of the Nelson family'.[4] The tall, red-haired Patrick was influencing history even in the opening hours of his university career. It would not be the only time he would touch history.

As the months passed, Patrick was to be associated with three great future historical figures. The College was named after St John the Evangelist and some recent graduates were deeply dedicated to the spread of the gospel that St John had famously written about. One was Henry Martyn (1781-1812) who had entered St John's Cambridge in the autumn of 1797 and was Senior Wrangler in 1801; it was regarded, at the time, as the greatest intellectual achievement obtainable in Britain.

To put it simply, the Senior Wrangler won the Cambridge University annual mathematics problem-solving competition and was accordingly recorded as their best undergraduate mathematician.

Martyn had intended to go to the Bar but, in October 1801, he heard Cambridge's most famous evangelical, the Rev Charles Simeon, speak of the great missionary work done by William Carey. Later, he was deeply influenced by reading the life of David Brainerd, the man known as the Apostle to the native Americans. Henry Martyn distinctly heard the call of God and set his heart on becoming a missionary.

Ordained into the Church of England ministry in October 1803, he served as the Rev Charles Simeon's curate at Holy Trinity, Cambridge. He left England for India in 1805 and served as a chaplain under the British East India Company. A brilliant linguist, in the remaining six years of his life, he translated the New Testament into Urdu, Hindi, Persian and Judaeo-Persic. He also revised an Arabic translation of the New Testament and translated the Psalms into Persian and the Prayer Book into Hindi. His diary has been called one of the most precious treasures of Anglican devotion. Martyn succumbed to illness and died in Tokat, Turkey on 16 October 1812. He was buried by strangers.

This much-beloved evangelical was approached by Patrick Brontë about eighteen months into his university career. In those months Patrick had worked very hard indeed. Patrick was a sitar, that is, a Cambridge undergraduate who had his tuition fees lowered and who was given free food. On top of this, by dent of college exhibitions and teaching pupils in his leisure hours he had managed to pay his bills. He had also become an outstanding scholar encouraged by great tutors. One of his tutors, James Wood, who later became Vice-Chancellor of

Cambridge University, had particularly encouraged and helped him.[5] The Cambridge University Calendars record that Patrick was one of only five men in his college career who maintained an unbroken record of first-class successes.[6]

Patrick, by 1804, had now fully committed himself to entering the Church of England ministry and approached Henry Martyn to see if he could gain some sponsorship from societies who helped young men preparing for ordination. Patrick was, despite all his hard work, in very real financial need. Martyn wrote to the Rev J Sargent (later his biographer), vicar of Graham in Sussex, of Patrick's dire financial straits.[7] Here, a fascinating line of contacts opened up into the very heart of history. It was 'networking' before the word had been invented.

A circle of friends in the Parish of Clapham near London, never more than twenty or thirty in number, had begun to emerge in English society. Later dubbed the Clapham Sect, they were anything but one. Led spiritually by the Rev John Venn, 'It is safe to say that never in the history of the church did the inhabitants of a single parish have such an effect on the world.'[8] For this group of Christians, good works were not limited to England. They intervened on behalf of the convicts of Australia, the victims of Napoleonic wars, the Greeks struggling for freedom, the Haitians, the North American Indians, the Hottentots and the African slave trade.

Right at the heart of this group was a young man who was to become, arguably, the most successful social reformer in history. He was a graduate of St John's College, Cambridge and a Yorkshire Member of Parliament who was one day to give what is reckoned to have been the greatest speech ever given in the House of Commons – it lasted for three-and-a-half hours!

Converted to Christ following his Cambridge days, he was encouraged to stay in Parliament by the Rev John Newton, the ex-slave captain famed for his hymn, *Amazing Grace*. He was slowly drawn into campaigning for the abolition of the slave trade and backed by his friend William Pitt, the youngest Prime Minister in British history. His crowning achievement was to be the abolition of the slave trade in 1807 and of slavery in the British Empire in 1833, just three days before his death. At one stage in his life, he was an active participant in an astonishing sixty-nine different public initiatives. 'He is no common Christian; his knowledge of divine things and the experience of the power of the gospel are very extraordinary,' wrote the Rev John Venn. His name was William Wilberforce.

Another member of the Clapham group was Henry Thornton, a cousin of William Wilberforce. Thornton was an outstanding economist, a leading British banker and a Member of Parliament. In 1802 he had written a work of great importance, *An Enquiry into the Nature of Efforts of the Paper Credit of Great Britain*; he has been called the father of the modern Central Bank. The Rev Sargent who was married to another cousin of William Wilberforce had, on receiving Henry Martyn's letter pleading Patrick Brontë's cause, got in touch with Henry Thornton on Patrick's behalf. Henry Thornton and William Wilberforce both agreed to sponsor Patrick Brontë through the rest of his university career.[9] The historian G M Trevelyan called the abolition of slavery 'one of the turning points in the history of the world'. Two men at the heart of it were not unmindful of the needs of the young man from Drumballyroney. Patrick was now touching history again, and how!

In writing to thank Wilberforce for the kindness shown, Henry Martyn made a very astute comment regarding what made Patrick Bronte tick. 'There is reason to hope,' he said, 'that he will be an instrument of good to the Church, as a desire of usefulness in the ministry seems to have influenced him hitherto in no small degree.'[10]

Again and again throughout Patrick's life the name of the Rev Charles Simeon surfaces. There is no question that this hugely influential evangelical figure impacted Patrick. He knew him and moved in his circle.[11] The Rev Henry Martyn was Simeon's curate at the time Patrick approached him for sponsorship. To understand where Patrick was coming from evangelically, it is very important to know something of Simeon.[12]

Here was a character of characters. As a freshman of King's College, Cambridge in January 1779, Simeon was required to take Holy Communion in King's College Chapel. To prepare himself he read the only religious book he had ever heard of, William Law's *Whole Duty of Man*. It led to a deep conviction of his need of personal faith in Christ. He made a great spiritual discovery. He wrote in his private memoir that, in Passion Week 1779, he asked himself: 'Has God provided an offering for me that I may lay my sins on his head? Then, God willing, I will not bear them on my own soul one moment longer. Accordingly, I sought to lay my sins upon the sacred head of Jesus; and on the Wednesday began to have a hope of mercy; on the Thursday that hope increased; on the Friday and Saturday it became more strong; and on the Sunday morning, Easter day, 4 April, I awoke early with these words upon my heart and lips, "Jesus Christ is risen today! Hallelujah! Hallelujah!" From that hour, peace flowed in rich abundance into my soul; and, at the Lord's Table in our Chapel, I had the sweetest access to God through my blessed Saviour.'

In 1782, Simeon became a Fellow of King's College and took Holy Orders in the Church of England. He received a living of

Holy Trinity, Cambridge in the following year. The parishioners, though, opposed Simeon's appointment, preferring a certain Rev Hammond and a most extraordinary state of affairs erupted. The parishioners had in their charge what was known as the Sunday Afternoon Lecturer. He addressed what was similar to a second Sunday service. Let Bishop Handley Moule take up the story:

'I need not explain how very unpopular the appointment was, it was very plainly shown to be so. The parishioners chose Hammond as Lecturer at once. By the usage of the office he thus had a right to the pulpit every Sunday afternoon, leaving only the morning to Simeon. That right he exercised for five years, and was then followed for seven years by another clergyman equally independent. Not till 1794 was the Minister chosen to be Lecturer also and on Sunday mornings the church for a long while was made as inaccessible as possible to him and his hearers. The pew doors were almost all locked and the should-be occupants were absent, leaving only the aisles for any congregation that might assemble. On the first Sunday, indeed, aisles and pews alike were nearly empty when the service began, a bitter trial for the lately popular young clergyman, but after a while people trooped in; and "multitudes" as the weeks went on were unable to find room. Simeon set forms in the aisles, and even put up open seats in nooks and corners at his own expense; but these the church wardens pulled down and threw into the churchyard.'

Stones were thrown at his church windows. It is recorded that, when walking in the streets, Simeon met with coarse abuse from idle undergraduates who thoroughly enjoyed hooting at him as late as 1820. Moule highlighted the fact that Simeon endured one of the most severe of all trials, social estrangement.

Simeon showed incredible Christian grace and patience through all of the abuse and opposition that he encountered. Taking as his guiding star Paul's advice to Timothy that 'the servant of the Lord must not strive' he turned the other cheek to his enemies. He was an awesome preacher who had a great open secret at the heart of his ministry, namely, his doctrine. It was, says Moule, two words: Jesus Christ. 'Everything in Simeon's preaching radiated from Jesus Christ and returned upon him.' Simeon had carved on the insides of his church pulpit where only he could see it, the words a group of Greeks spoke to St Philip: 'Sir,' they said, 'we would see Jesus.' (John 12:1)

Slowly, ever so slowly, the tide of opposition began to turn. Simeon, incredibly, stayed by his task at Holy Trinity for fifty-four years to become one of the greatest influences on the life of the English church and the spread of the gospel worldwide. He helped bring into existence the British and Foreign Bible Society and the Church Missionary Society and he administered the appointment of chaplains in the East India Company. It is said that, by the time he died, one-third of all Anglican ministers in the country had sat under his teaching at one time or another. His published sermons are still in print. He established the Simeon Trust for the purpose of acquiring church patronage to perpetuate evangelical clergy in the Church of England parishes which continues to operate to this day.

He was buried in King's College Chapel on 19 November 1836 and 'the whole university was resolved to honour this man, once almost banished from its society.' It was a Saturday and 'the town was busy with the market; but all the shops in the main street were shut, and the iron railings east and north of the college were beset by dense crowds of people. In the university and colleges almost every lecture that morning was suspended that all who might could go to the grave. It is no dishonour to other illustrious names to say that probably Cambridge never saw such a funeral as Simeon's. More than 1,500 gownsmen attended. Every bell of the college chapels tolled for him. Heads of houses, doctors, professors, men of all ages, stations and opinions and of every college came to his burial.'

On his deathbed Simeon had said to his friends that the text which comforted him was: 'In the beginning God created the heavens and the earth!' That surprised them until he explained 'why, if out of nothing, God can bring all the wonders of the world, he may yet make something out of me!' He certainly did just that and Patrick Brontë was one of the beneficiaries.

Drawing from a letter written many years later by Charlotte Brontë, Juliet Barker suggests that Patrick 'seems to have been one of those ardent young men who met in Simeon's rooms and [who] were taught the necessity of preaching to humble the sinner, to exalt the Saviour and to promote holiness.'[13] Patrick's sails were by now carefully set for an evangelical ministry on the tides of English history.

Those tides were being threatened in the summer of 1803 by an invasion flotilla being organised by a tyrant. Napoleon Bonaparte had continued to interfere in Italy and Switzerland and Great Britain had declared war on France back in May. It was no idle threat that lay across the Channel and the British Government called for Volunteers. Patrick volunteered and joined the 4th Division of Volunteers Corps made up of men from St John's and Peterhouse College. For nine months they drilled and trained in the Market Square of Cambridge under the command of an eighteen-year-old St John's student called Viscount Palmerston, who had been elected Officer in Charge.[14] Everywhere Patrick seemed to turn he was touching history and he would always be proud to say in later years that he had drilled at Cambridge under the man who was to serve twice as Prime Minister in the mid-nineteenth century.

Patrick's four years of fastidious study at Cambridge came to an end when on St George's Day, 23 April 1806, he formally graduated with a Bachelor of Arts degree. The day before he took an oath to abide by the Thirty-Nine Articles of the Church of England. He was ordained a Deacon in Holy Orders in London on 10 August having by then been appointed curate in the Parish of Wethersfield in Essex, about 35 miles from Cambridge.[15]

Patrick's youngest sister, Alice, told of Patrick returning to Drumballyroney Parish Church in Ireland before taking up his curacy at Wethersfield to preach one of his first sermons. The congregation must, indeed, have been an inquisitive one. No doubt, the Rev William Tighe would have warmly welcomed Patrick home and his youngest sister, Alice, told of how 'all our old friends and neighbours were there, and the church was very full ... he preached a gran' sermon, and never had anything in his han' the whole time.'[16]

One can imagine his family and former pupils and neighbours and friends crowding in to see if 'Pat Prunty' had changed any. What was his text? What was his theme? What was the conversation as those farming folk filed out that Sunday morning so long ago?

One thing was certain. There was no hint that this was to be the father of one of the most incredible literary families in history. Few people heading home for lunch that Sunday, in the shadow of the Mountains of Mourne, would have realised that three of Patrick's daughters would one day examine Christian doctrine and ethics with their pens in such a unique and unforgettable way.

THREE

Life is Not Tidy

AMIDST ALL of Patrick Brontë's university career no sign appears that he ever fell in love. His head was in his books and his heart was set on the Christian ministry. When he took up that ministry in a little village in Essex in October 1806 it took a farmer's daughter called Mary Burder to lift that studious head and to stir that dedicated heart towards thoughts of love and marriage.

One day, amidst his busy duties, Patrick walked into the kitchen of St George's House where he lodged opposite St Mary Magdalene Parish Church[1] and there stood the intelligent, affectionate, kind, forgiving, agreeable and pretty Mary Burder preparing dinner. Mary had been sent over to her aunt's house where Patrick lodged with a gift of some game. The thirty-year-old Patrick and the eighteen-year-old Mary were instantly attracted to each other. Their friendship grew with walks around the woods to Mary's home at The Broad, a mile away, and Mary shared with Patrick an interest in books. He even loaned her some of his. Mary's father had died shortly before Patrick arrived at Wethersfield and her uncle who lived nearby had become her guardian.[2]

Patrick, soon deeply in love, proposed marriage to Mary and she accepted.[3] Patrick, though, soon ran into a storm. Mary's family opposed the marriage and she was under the legal age to marry without consent. Her uncle took her to his house in Great Yeldham to prevent any more walks by the woods or any other private meetings between them. To preach in his pulpit at St Mary Magdalene, Wethersfield and to minister in the parish at weddings, funerals, christenings and Sunday services cannot have been easy.

Looking at all the evidence from Patrick and Mary's letters to and from each other it seems that it was Patrick who ended the engagement. He was in deep turmoil and anguish over the whole situation as his letters to his friend, the Rev John Munn, prove.[4] There was, of course, the social and religious divide between them which, in those times, was significant. Mary was not a member of the Church of England but attended the Congregational Chapel in the village. This would have caused real problems for Patrick's future career as a minister within the Church of England. It appears that Patrick took the family's opposition to his marriage to Mary as guidance from God and broke off the engagement.[5]

Mary later wrote understandably sarcastically in a letter to Patrick in 1823, when he tried to renew friendship with her, that 'happily for me I have not been the ascribed cause of hindering your promotion, of preventing any brilliant alliance, nor have those great and affluent friends that you used to write and speak of withheld their patronage on my account, young, inexperienced, unsuspecting and ignorant as I then was of what I had a right to look forward to.'[6] Mary had been wounded and Patrick had been traumatised. The truth was he had acted too hastily. It was not a great start to his career as a clergyman. Four days before Christmas, in December 1807, he was ordained as an Anglican Priest in the august Chapel Royal of St James, Westminster. One lesson was very clear to him: life is anything but tidy.

All this turmoil led Patrick to seek another post which he found at All Saints Parish Church, Wellington, Shropshire. He became curate to the Simeon-influenced evangelical rector, John Eyton, a St John's College graduate. The registers of the church showed that Patrick was now adding an accent to his name: it now appeared as Brontë.[7]

Patrick again found himself at the heart of the reforming evangelicals of his generation. The Rev Eyton had transformed the Wellington Free School into a model of its time in providing education for poor children. The curate, the Rev William Morgan, whom Patrick replaced had been rector of Madeley six miles from Wellington. Patrick became friends with Morgan and was now introduced to the famed evangelical circle of the great writer and preacher, John Fletcher of Madeley.[8]

Fletcher was a close friend of the Wesley brothers, John and Charles. Of him, John Wesley said, 'He had not known his equal for godliness and holiness of life.' His widow Mary still welcomed her husband's friends to her home. There is no doubt that the aged and saintly Mary and her circle were close to the Methodist influence. This, of course, had already been embraced by Patrick in Drumballyroney and from his mentor, William Tighe. It must have been a 'balm in Gilead' to the broken-hearted Patrick to be spiritually enfolded by these sincere and godly Christians.

Patrick, though, was not destined to be drawn into a permanent ministry in the beautiful county of which A E Housman wrote in his poem, *A Shropshire Lad*:

Loveliest of trees, the cherry now
Is hung with bloom along the bough,
And stands about the woodland ride
Wearing white for Eastertide.

Now, of my threescore years and ten,
Twenty will not come again,
And take from seventy springs a score,
It only leaves me fifty more.

And since to look at things in bloom
Fifty springs are little room,
About the woodlands I will go
To see the cherry hung with snow.[9]

Patrick's heart lay in Yorkshire and away from the wide Severn's waters. He felt that Yorkshire offered him great opportunities for the spread of the Christian gospel and the Rev John Buckworth, vicar of Dewsbury near Bradford, was looking for an evangelical assistant. Patrick was offered the position.

As Patrick contemplated a call to Dewsbury, he received a letter from his former tutor, James Wood, offering him the post of serving as chaplain to the Governor of Martinique in the West Indies.[10] Martinique had recently been taken from the French in the Napoleanic wars and it offered Patrick a whole new world. Twenty-four years later 800,000 slaves were to be freed in the

West Indies as a result of the William Wilberforce-led campaign in the House of Commons. Patrick, obviously, had the opportunity to be part of that campaign in the West Indies from a highly prestigious position. He was touching history again but now decided that it was better for him to serve God in Yorkshire. On such decisions, literary history also swings.

Patrick's eighteen-month ministry at Dewsbury was anything but idle. He conducted dozens of weddings, baptisms and, sadly, many funerals. He helped lead Yorkshire's very first Sunday School.[11] He actually rescued a boy from drowning after he had been pushed into the River Calder. As the boy was being swept away in the current, Patrick plunged in and rescued him.[12] Patrick also campaigned successfully through his contact with Wilberforce and he, in turn, through Lord Palmerston, on behalf of a wrongly-accused soldier.[13]

In 1811, Patrick moved as curate to Hartshead, four miles from Dewsbury, and it was in this parish that he published his *Cottage Poems*. Patrick drew great pleasure from writing poetry and sought through his poems to convey the message of Christ's gospel. In his preaching he insisted on the importance of an inward, personal conversion brought about by faith in Christ alone for salvation.

The following words from one of his sermons bears this out: 'Constant and regular attendance at church and a strict conformity to every Christian rite and ceremony is no positive proof that a man is a child of God. Under these circumstances, he may still continue ignorant of divine truths ... to be a genuine Christian and in a state of salvation, it is necessary, not only that we should be outwardly moral, but that our morality should spring from faith in Christ.'[14]

While at Hartshead the famous Luddite rebellion erupted on Patrick's watch.[15] A combination of dire poverty, war, unemployment and the introduction of new textile machinery forcing cottage-based industries out of business led to deep unrest in the West Riding of Yorkshire. The Luddites attacked new machines being brought across Hartshead Moor in February 1812, followed by attacks on mills in the Huddersfield area where machines were smashed. On the night of 11 April a large force of Luddites, drawn from across Patrick's parish, attacked Rawfolds Mill near Hartshead. The mill was guarded and, in the ensuing shooting, two men were killed. The Luddites withdrew.   Later, a woollen manufacturer called William Marsden was ambushed and murdered.   This all led to executions.[16]

In the midst of this turmoil, Patrick was in love again. There might have been Luddites to the left of him and Luddites to his right and even in front of him on Sunday's but he had fallen for the daughter of a prosperous grocer and tea merchant from Penzance in Cornwall. Patrick's friend, the Rev John Fennell, had been appointed headmaster of a new Boarding School at Woodhouse Grove at Rawdon near Bradford.   Fennell's wife, assisted by their daughter Jane, was matron and housekeeper.

Patrick was invited over to examine the boys in Classics and to give a report to the school committee. It was on this occasion that he was introduced to Fennell's niece by marriage, the twenty-nine-year-old Maria Branwell, who was also helping her aunt run the school.[17] This time the path of love ran much more smoothly. From a strong Wesleyan family, one of Maria's most memorable characteristics to come down to us today is her wit. This is shown very clearly in her letters to Patrick, which he carefully preserved.

Deeply committed to the Christian cause, Maria was as certain as Patrick that God had brought them together. In the month of their wedding, December 1812, she wrote: 'I am certain no one ever loved you with an affection more pure, constant, tender and ardent than that which I feel ... oh, let us pray much for wisdom and grace to fill our appointed stations with propriety, that we may enjoy satisfaction in our souls, edify others, and bring glory to the name of him who has wonderfully preserved, blessed, and brought us together.'[18]

It was a double wedding because Patrick's friend, the Rev William Morgan, now a vicar in Bradford, had been courting Jane Fennell at the same time as Patrick had been courting Maria. The weddings took place at Guiseley Parish Church on 29 December 1812.[19] William solemnised the marriage of Patrick and Maria and immediately afterwards Patrick solemnised the marriage of William and Jane.

Patrick and Maria had no inkling that day that one of their daughters would create fiction's most famous wedding ceremony and in it awesomely defend Christian marriage. The story of Jane Eyre and Rochester, though, were the literary product of the values being expounded in Guiseley that day by the Irish clergyman. The 1812 overture by Pyotr Ilyich Tchaikovsky famously commemorates the unsuccessful invasion of Napoleon into Russia and the devastating retreat from Moscow of his Grande Armée that had occurred three months previously. The weddings at Guiseley in Yorkshire four days after Christmas in the same year was an overture to extraordinary literature.

Love and marriage made a deep impression on Patrick's literary life in the months following. In September 1813 he published *The Rural Minstrel: A Miscellany of Descriptive Poems* containing eleven poems in all. Full of deep appreciation for the beauties of nature, Patrick's poems reflect his passionate belief that nature reflects the Creator. He was no pantheist.

As roves my mind, o'er nature's works abroad,
It sees, reflected, their creative God,
The insects, dancing in the sunny beam,
Whose filmy wings, like golden atoms gleam,
The finny tribe, that glance across the lake,
The timid hare, that rustles through the brake,
The squirrel blithe, that frisks on yonder spray,
The wily fox, that prowls about for prey,
Have each a useful lesson for my heart,
And sooth(e) my soul, and rural sweets impart.[20]

One can only imagine the joy at the birth of little Maria Brontë, christened on 23 April 1814.[21]   Another daughter, Elizabeth, arrived on 8 February 1815.   In May of that memorable year Patrick and his young family moved to serve God in the parish of Thornton, four miles from the centre of Bradford.

About four weeks later the most momentous battle of the nineteenth century raged in Belgium, far from Patrick's Christian ministry in Yorkshire.   It was to cost the British General, the Duke of Wellington, around 15,000 of his men dead and wounded; Napoleon Bonaparte, the Emperor of the French, 25,000; and the Prussians, under Field Marshal Blucher, around 7,000.   It was to be one of the most pivotal battles in world history and its victor was to be an often-mentioned hero in the Brontë family for the rest of their lives.

FOUR

Indescribable Pleasure and Sufficient Grace

ON 23 JULY 1815, the Rev Patrick Brontë led a service of thanksgiving in Thornton for the victory won by his fellow Irishman, the Duke of Wellington, at the Battle of Waterloo. His sermon on the day is not on record but it must have been fascinating to listen to. Collections were taken in his church for the widows and orphans of those fallen in battle.[1] The demise of Napoleon as the scourge of Europe brought international rejoicing.

Patrick's stay in Thornton was marked by some very significant events in the life of his family. The first was literary. In a magazine called *The Pastoral Visitor* he wrote a short story on the subject of conversion, published in three parts. As he pointed out in a letter to the editor, the work concentrates on the 'views and feelings of an awakened sinner before he got proper notion of the all sufficiency of Christ.'[2]

He also wrote another story which was later to be published as a little book entitled, *The Cottage in the Wood* subtitled, *Or The Art of Becoming Rich and Happy.*[3] The story of Mary and the drunken and wealthy rake who pursues her is fascinating in that it is a seedbed for later Brontë novels. Mary refused to be the rake's mistress or wife because of his atheism and immorality but, on his conversion to Christ, Mary marries him and they both go on to know much happiness.

Shades *of Jane Eyre* emerge at the parsonage of Thornton and *The Cottage in the Wood* is the first book to bare the name Brontë on its title page. Fascinatingly, the now famous diaeresis in the name Brontë appears for the first time. It seems that it came as a result of a printing error because it does not appear in any of Patrick's signatures in his correspondence or registers at the time; there he was still using Brontē.[4]

Patrick's wife Maria also wrote an article on conversion and education that does not seem to have been published.[5] Three other very important events occurred at Thornton. On 21 April 1816, Maria gave birth to a baby girl named after her youngest sister, Charlotte. On 26 June 1817, great joy and a deeply-fulfilled wish came to the Thornton parsonage in the birth of Patrick and Maria's first son, Branwell, who took his mother's maiden name.

Patrick's pen did not lie idle. In April 1818, Patrick's *The Maid of Killarney* was published.[6] Its depiction of Ireland as an island of tragic beauty is highlighted in Patrick's descriptions of its physical beauty and dire poverty. The book is a love story carrying an evangelical message. It also highlights Patrick's abhorrence of the Roman Catholic Church's policy in those days of discouraging the laity from reading the Scriptures for themselves. He also discusses Roman Catholic Emancipation. He opposes Roman Catholics being allowed to vote or to sit in Parliament on the basis that Papal loyalty would overwhelm loyalty to the King. He later changed his mind on the subject. The book also calls for an overhauling of the system of criminal justice highlighted by the anomaly that 'a man will be hanged for stealing a fat sheep, though he be hungry; he will incur no greater punishment for murdering twenty men!'[7]

The Maid of Killarney was to hugely influence Patrick's children and they were to lift the character of Flora in the novel as a model for the heroines they wrote of in their youth. The Duke of Wellington, much praised by Patrick in the novel, later became a great hero of Charlotte's. Patrick had written in his *Cottage Poems* of the 'indescribable pleasure' he received from the act of literary composition. He was to pass that pleasure on to his girls who were to touch the world with the result and who were to bring 'indescribable pleasure' to millions who have since read their work. One of those amazing daughters of Patrick's appeared on 30 July 1818. She was named Emily Jane Brontë.

Patrick had a good ministry at Thornton marked by dedication to his calling and kindness shown to his people. It was, though, to experience what one could only call a huge disturbance. The row over the appointment of Patrick's hero, the Rev Charles Simeon, to Holy Trinity, Cambridge was to foreshadow the next big event in his life.

In May 1819, the Rev Henry Heap, the vicar of Bradford, offered Patrick the incumbency of Haworth in Yorkshire. Patrick was delighted and believed that God had called him to the parish. With five children, and another one on the way, and facing very real financial difficulties, he was also glad of the better living it promised. The promise though became overwhelmed by in-fighting between the church trustees at Haworth and the church authorities at Bradford.

It all went back to Elizabethan times. The vicars of Bradford had the right to nominate and appoint the living of Haworth but, from the time of Elizabeth l, the trustees had the right to pay the salary of the vicars of Haworth. If they declined to pay the vicar's salary there would be trouble and trouble there was.

The trustees of Haworth church had nothing personal against Patrick but they wholly resisted the fact that the vicars of Bradford had forced him on them! Patrick tried to resign but the Church authorities made it very clear to him that he would be in trouble with the Archbishop if he did. Eventually, he wrote a letter of resignation to both the vicar of Bradford and the Archbishop. The trustees at Haworth then offered to consider nominating Patrick themselves if he would go to Haworth and preach. Patrick refused and told them they could come to hear him at Thornton!

On 8 October 1818, the Archbishop of York wrote to Patrick ordering him to take the services at Haworth the following Sunday. It must have been a rough ride for Patrick because on 19 January his formal resignation was finally accepted.

Patrick's friend, the Rev Samuel Redhead, was now appointed. On his first Sunday, 31 October, a congregation of five hundred gathered and on a given signal, just as Redhead entered the pulpit, the whole congregation rose and left the church shouting, 'Come out, come out!' Redhead was pursued and mocked and insulted.

The next Sunday the congregation did the same thing again, this time laughing, talking, leaping over pews, stamping their feet and shouting. All this while the poor vicar tried to conduct prayers. Following this disgraceful behaviour, the besieged vicar had to conduct a funeral service, which was given relative silence and then the crowd turned on the vicar and pursued him out of Haworth with mockery, shoving and pushing, shouting and insult.

The Archbishop of York now threatened to shut the church and bring the situation to the Lord Chancellor. The next Sunday the intrepid and brave Redhead returned to Haworth and was met with the same shouting, insulting crowd who accompanied him all the way to the church. Their indecent behaviour continued inside the church during the service and Redhead had to close it. He gave direction that the church should be shut up until instructions were received from the Archbishop. Protected by the churchwardens, he was pursued out of town for over one-and-a-half miles by a crowd which he described as being more 'like wild beasts than human beings'. The next day he wrote to the Archbishop and had his resignation accepted.[8]

Patrick Brontë must have heard news of all this behaviour with trepidation. *The Leeds Intelligencer* fired a very public broadside against the people of Haworth. They said the behaviour was 'scarcely possible in a heathen village' and that 'the church wardens are certainly liable to a prosecution for the wilful neglect of their duty and deserve to feel, that the house of God, and the hallowed ground of a churchyard are not proper places in which to allow by disturbance and howlings, the loudest and lowest marks of irreverence and insult.'[9] Patrick had to go to Haworth to perform two funerals, a christening and a marriage across following days.

It was into such an intense environment that Patrick and Maria's last child, Anne, was born on 17 January 1820. It is little wonder that she grew up to understand the world of nineteenth century Anglican clergyman so well.

At this time the Archbishop of York decided that a meeting should be held between the vicar of Bradford and the trustees of

Haworth. The outcome, after noisy argument, was that the trustees and the vicar of Bradford should jointly offer the nomination to the Rev Patrick Brontë. The family moved to Haworth in April where all their earthly goods had been moved in two flat wagons.[10] Millions of people were one day to visit Haworth for the sole reason that the Brontës had moved there. The town would never be the same again.

Spiritually, the Haworth that Patrick Brontë entered had been deeply affected by an extraordinary vicar fifty years before. His work had left a huge evangelical legacy. His name was William Grimshaw. In June 1742, there were but twelve communicants in the Anglican Church in Haworth. In less than six months after Grimshaw arrived there was an incredible spiritual awakening. As Grimshaw put it: 'In 1742, our dear Lord was pleased to visit my parish.' Within a year the church with only twelve communicants was crowded with over nine hundred people and many more standing outside. Hundreds of people came across the surrounding moors to see what was going on. Grimshaw took out a window on the north side of the church near his three-decker pulpit and erected scaffolding. This enabled him to step on to the outside platform at times during his sermons to help those people gathered in the churchyard to hear him better! A great man of prayer and praise with a sincere love of his people, Grimshaw was marked by outstanding generosity.

Some years into his ministry, Archbishop John Gibbert arrived at Haworth for a confirmation service with other clergy. He had a word with Grimshaw in private and discussed with him, amongst other complaints, that his sermons were 'very loose and he could and did preach about everything.' The Archbishop gave him a text and said that he wished to hear him preach on it in two hours time. Grimshaw is reported to have looked out the vestry door and seeing an expectant crowd asked why they should have to wait two hours. He went into the church, prayed fervent extempore prayers for the Archbishop, and launched into his sermon. After the people had left, the clergy waited to hear the verdict. Gibbert took Grimshaw by the arm and, with a tremor in his voice, said: 'I wish to God that all the clergy in my diocese were like this good man.'

In 1747, Charles Wesley preached in Haworth during Grimshaw's ministry and, after he had opened in prayer, the crowd of up to four thousand people outside begged him to come out and preach to them. There were even clutches of people in the lead ceiling joints on the roof and the steeple. The great George Whitfield, arguably the most eloquent of all eighteenth century ministers, preached often from Grimshaw's scaffolding outside the south wall. It became known as Whitfield's pulpit.

On one occasion he announced his Bible text: 'It is appointed unto men once to die but after this the judgment' (Hebrews 9:27). There was a loud shriek and a person dropped dead in his huge congregation. He announced his text again and there was another loud shriek and yet another person dropped dead. The Countess of Huntingdon, a friend of evangelicals who was present, begged Whitfield not to announce the text a third time.

Perhaps the most famous recorded statement between Whitfield and Grimshaw was when Whitfield in his sermon implied that the people of Haworth under Grimshaw's ministry should know the gospel. Grimshaw shouted out: 'Oh sir! For God's sake do not speak so! I pray you do not flatter them! I fear the greater part of them are going to hell with their eyes open.'

Grimshaw's excessive zeal, though, went to a serious extreme. He would announce a psalm at the Sunday service and then go out and drive reluctant parishioners into church with a horsewhip. People at times could be seen on a Sunday jumping from the windows of the *Black Bull* in Haworth not because there was a fire but because the parson was after them! For all his idiosyncrancies and extremes this was the same man who asked for cast-off boots, paid for them to be repaired, and gave them to the poor. He constantly took food from his own table to feed the hungry. When he died on 8 April 1763 he was genuinely and deeply mourned.[11]

Mrs Gaskill in her biography of Charlotte Brontë has written in depth of Grimshaw and of the wildness of the Haworth he inhabited. She wrote that the old custom of 'arvills' or funeral feasts of the time, led to frequent pitched battles between the drunken mourners. 'There were,' she writes, 'horse races held on the moors just above the village which were periodical sources of drunkenness and profligacy.' She adds: 'Scarcely a wedding took place without the rough amusement of foot-races where the half-naked runners were a scandal to all decent strangers.' All in all, the environment of Haworth was much improved by the work of the Rev Grimshaw. 'Even now,' wrote Mrs Gaskill in the time of Patrick Brontë, 'the memory of this good man is held in reverence and his faithful ministrations and real virtues are one of the boasts of the parish.'[12]

Mrs Gaskill gives the impression in her biography of Charlotte Brontë that Haworth has little changed since Grimshaw's day. Here is a world of coarseness, drunkenness, and profligacy still. All this she insists is grist to the mill of Emily's novel, *Wuthering Heights*, and Anne's novel, *The Tenant of Wildfell Hall*. It all feeds into Charlotte's depiction of the profligate Mr Rochester. This has also fed the myth of the genius of the Brontë family in Haworth 'growing up in physical and social isolation, excluded from all normal preoccupations of ordinary life, let alone genteel society.'[13]

Juliet Barker has brilliantly demythologised this picture. She proves that the Haworth of the Brontë days was a very different place to that of Grimshaw's. It was now a township transformed by the industrial revolution. Constant traffic from the wool trade passed through the town and the ample water supply in Haworth, situated in the hills above Keighley and Bradford, fed thirteen small textile mills along the River Worth by the time Patrick and his family arrived.[14] Haworth ran its own worsted trade and quarrying went on in the surrounding hills.[15] It had its own resident surgeon, wine and spirit merchant, watchmaker, five butchers, two confectioners, eleven grocers, three cabinet makers and six public houses also provided rooms and dinners.[16] All this was surrounded by the beautiful sweep of moorlands surrounding the town, now famed across the world by the Brontë sisters who caught it in prose.

Soon Patrick was hard at work in his new, improved parish preaching in St Michael's and All Angels Parish Church under the texts Grimshaw had placed on the sounding board above his famous three-tiered pulpit: 'For I determined not to know anything among you, save Jesus Christ and him crucified' (1 Corinthians 2:2) and 'For to me to live is Christ, and to die is gain' (Philippians 1:21).[17] He also gave himself wholeheartedly to the care and defence of the poor in his parish.

It must have been with high hopes and deep determination that Patrick turned in his ministry to the new year of 1821. It began sadly when he had to officiate at the funeral of his friend, John Firth, on 2 January over at Thornton.[18] At the end of the month, one of the most devastating blows of his life horrendously struck his home. Right out of the blue, his wife Maria took dangerously ill with internal cancer. Frantic and beside himself with grief, Patrick did every earthly thing open to him to care for his dying wife. He called in the best medical help available, he bought medicines, he employed a nurse, and personally nursed his wife through the long dark nights of her distressing suffering.[19] Daily, he unflinchingly carried on with his duties as a minister of Jesus Christ in his Haworth parish conducting the burial services for sixty-two people during her seven-and-a-half month illness.[20]

Being in a new parish Patrick deeply missed his many friends of past days. People did help but the situation grew immeasurably darker when three of Patrick's children went down with scarlet fever in one day. The following day his other three children succumbed to the same illness which is transmitted through coughing or sneezing. Mainly cured today by penicillin, in Patrick's day scarlet fever was usually fatal.

As Patrick's wife lay fatally ill, he later described what he went through as 'the greatest load of sorrows that ever pressed on me.'[21] He must have viewed the flushed faces and the fevered brows of his children with horror. The rapid pulses, the vomiting, the abdominal pains, the bright red tongues, the fine red rashes, all seemed a death knell to him of what was incalculably precious. He seemed on the brink of losing all his children and their mother at one and the same time. Here was a man who was constantly assisting the bereaved all across his adult life, standing by gravesides quoting the comforting verses found in Scripture. Now every hour that passed seemed to bring him closer to having to attend the funeral services of his own loved ones.

Mercifully, the rashes on his children's bodies began to fade. Never was Patrick happier to see flakes peeling from the face and hands of any child for the rest of his life. Those flakes were the sign of returning health. Soon to Patrick's great relief,

Maria's sister Elizabeth arrived from Cornwall to help in the crisis. Death, as 1 Corinthians 15:26 declares, is the last enemy that will be destroyed and death was very busy.

Now Patrick's mentor was taken, the Rev Thomas Tighe, rector of Drumballyroney in Ireland. The man who had enormously helped Patrick toward the Christian ministry would no longer be there for him. He must now seek to hold the torch of the Christian faith high despite the ever-encroaching darkness of sorrow.

The torch must have trembled in his hand on many a day, as Patrick put it, 'death pursued [Maria] unrelentingly.'[22] Maria must have been in unbelievable agony. 'Oh God, my poor children; oh God, my poor children!' she kept crying.[23] Patrick described her death on 15 September 1821, thus: 'Her constitution was enfeebled, and her frame wasted daily; and after about seven months of more agonising pain than I ever saw anyone endure, she fell asleep in Jesus, and her soul took its flight to the mansions of glory. During many years she walked with God; but the great enemy, envying her of holiness, often disturbed her mind in the last conflict. Still, in general, she had peace and joy in believing; and died, if not triumphantly, at least calmly, and with a holy, yet humble confidence that Christ was her Saviour, and heaven her eternal home.'[24] She was thirty-eight years old.

It is obvious from this statement that Patrick was shaken by his wife's faith being so shaken by approaching death. Evangelicals in Patrick's day, one feels, tended to forget, as they still often do, that the Lord Jesus was actually angry at the death of his friend, Lazarus. The Greek word *embrimaomai,* used twice in St John's Gospel to describe his reaction, means 'to snort as a horse does with anger' (John 11:33, 38). Christ was angry at what death had done to his friend for this was not how it was meant to be. It is no sin to be angry in the face of death as Christ was. There is triumph in Christ because he raised Lazarus from the dead. This triumph is, though, as shown in the life of Christ, balanced by the admission of reality. Patrick would have been better advised to admit to that reality.

When Maria died, all of her children, aged seven downwards, were standing at the bottom of her bed.[25] Words are inadequate to describe the scene. For fifteen days Patrick was unable to perform his duties as a minister. He was completely devastated. His friend, the Rev William Morgan, officiated at Maria's funeral on 22 September 1821 and she was buried in the vault near the altar under Haworth church.[26]

Patrick Brontë had his faults but no one can accuse him of being insincere in his Christian faith. He needed it now more than ever. He wrote: 'And when my dear wife was dead, and buried, and gone, and when I missed her at every corner, and when her memory was hourly revived by the innocent yet distressing prattle of my children, I do assure you, my dear Sir, from what I felt, I was happy in the recollection, that to sorrow, not as those without hope, was no sin; that our Lord himself had wept over his departed friend, and that he had promised us grace and strength sufficient for such a day.'[27]

As Patrick lived daily within sight of the church building where his gentle and godly wife was buried and as he turned to take up his ministry once more, he would need Christ's promised grace and sufficient strength more than he would ever have imagined.

FIVE

Indifferent Writing

WHEN PATRICK Brontë proposed to the twenty-four-year-old Elizabeth Firth of Kipping House in Thornton scarcely three months after Maria's death, distaste was not the word to describe her reaction. Anger erupted in the heart and mind of the godmother of some of his children.[1] How could he? It did not help things any that she was being courted by the Rev James Clarke Franks, a St John's College, Cambridge graduate. She decided to have nothing more to do with the Brontës. Thankfully, after her marriage to the Rev Franks, she relented her decision, two years later.[2]

Patrick though, helped financially after Maria's death by his friends, must have been a deeply disturbed clergyman. It is easy to believe the myth that he became a half-mad eccentric and recluse if Mrs Gaskell's account of him in her biography of

Charlotte is to be believed. One believed it oneself until one read Juliet Barker's brave and meticulously researched defence of Patrick's character. We owe her a great debt for putting Patrick's reputation to rights. She shows that some of Mrs Gaskell's apocryphal stories of Patrick were based on those told by what seems to have been a begrudged servant whom he had dismissed.

Juliet Barker proves that Patrick was not the bad-tempered father whose six children were 'grave and silent beyond their years' slipping around the house spiritlessly and noiselessly.[3] She does it by particularly drawing from the testimony of Nancy Garrs, Patrick's cook and assistant housekeeper who, with her sister Sarah, the nursemaid, was devoted to the family even long after she left their service.[4] She also highlights the writing of Patrick's friend, William Dearden, who took up his defence against the lies told about him in the pages of the *Bradford Observer*.[5]

Nancy denied the stories told of Patrick venting anger by sawing the backs of chairs, burning a hearth rug in the fire, and of burning the coloured boots belonging to his children to stop 'love of dress'. She also denied the stories told of Patrick giving his children vegetarian meals and further working of his anger or displeasure by firing his pistols out the back door. Nor was he the eccentric scholar-preacher shut up in his study and never sharing meals with his children. He ate regularly with them, took them on rambles, and showed them kindness and love. He was even involved in their games, which consisted of far more activity than the portrait Mrs Gaskell gives of them all sitting timidly listening to Maria reading the newspapers. Here were happy, romping, zestful children who walked on the moors most days, their peals of laughter audible to all who passed them.[6] Patrick talked to his children after tea in the evenings, giving them lessons in history, biography and travel, while the girls sewed. They drew from those lessons in the little plays they enacted as well as from the information-packed newspapers that came into their home, read to them by Maria, the eldest child in the family. On Sunday evenings, Patrick gathered all his children around him, including his servants, for Bible study and catechism.

Elizabeth Branwell, Maria's sister, promised to stay at the rectory until the children went to school. An affectionate and good woman, she made a huge sacrifice of easier and better times amongst her friends in Penzance in order to stay with the Brontë family. She must have been an absolute mainstay to Patrick.

Amid the deep snows of the winter of 1822 it is said that Patrick proposed to Isabella Drury, the sister of the vicar of Keighley. There is clear evidence that if he did she would not have countenanced it.[7] Whatever is thought of the Irish father of the Brontë family of Howarth, it is certainly clear that in the matter of proposing marriage he was not easily discouraged. He, now, of all things, turned back to Mary Burton, the girl of his Wethersfield dreams, fourteen years previously. He hoped there might still be a spark of love for him in her heart that he might encourage to a flame.

Patrick wrote to Mary's mother hoping to find out if she had married.[8] As it turned out, he got a letter from Mary herself which unequivocally informed him that she had no desire whatsoever to renew acquaintance with him. Undaunted, Patrick wrote back trying his best to woo her and telling her he wished for an opportunity to make amends for any pain he had caused her by '... attention and kindness'.[9] Mary would have none of it and in her last letter to him hoped he would be as faithful, zealous and successful in his Haworth ministry as the

Rev William Grimshaw had been. She put the knife in by telling him the Lord could supply all his and his children's needs![10]

Patrick's next letter asking for pardon for any wrong done seems to have gone unanswered.[11] It looked as though Patrick was going to have to go it alone. His attempt to turn back the clock failed. Anyone with any touch of empathy, though, could understand that life must have been incredibly lonely and difficult for him. It was to get much, much worse.

Patrick's future sorrow turned on a newspaper advertisement for a new Clergy Daughters' School at Cowan Bridge, southeast of Kirby Lonsdale in Lancashire.[12] The fees were less than those of Crofton Hall, near Wakefield, where he had sent his oldest daughters, Maria and Elizabeth. Patrons of the school included revered evangelicals like William Wilberforce, Hannah More and Charles Simeon. The headmaster, the Rev Carus Wilson, a well-known evangelical preacher, seemed to be the very man to oversee the school and the future education of Patrick's daughters. He moved Maria and Elizabeth to Cowan Bridge in July 1824 and Charlotte, one month later.

In the school's Admissions Register it was noted that Charlotte Brontë 'writes indifferently' and 'knows nothing of grammar'. It was also noted that Charlotte 'although clever for her age' knew 'nothing systematically'.[13] Before Charlotte's pen would lie unused forever, Cowan Bridge School would be immortalised as Lowood School in *Jane Eyre*.

There is no more damming condemnation of the extremes of unbalanced evangelicalism in world literature. Few read it without a shudder. The story of Helen Burns and her life and death at Lowood School haunt the reader of *Jane Eyre* long after reading of the repentance of Mr Rochester. If Charlotte Brontë was an 'indifferent writer' when she entered Cowan Bridge School, she soon lost her indifference when she remembered her school experiences and wrote her way through to be part of the greatest fiction writing, ever.

That the long-suffering, persecuted Helen Burns was, as Charlotte seemed to later suggest to her literary editor, a fictional cover for her sister Maria, makes the story even more haunting.[14] Comparing Maria's life and death to Helen Burns there are too many parallels to be coincidental. That Charlotte stated that she 'abstained from recording much that I remember respecting her, lest the narrative should sound incredible' makes one shudder even more.[15] Few former pupil's pens have dipped into ink more effectively to damn their former school. That the Cowan Bridge School was run in the name of Christ is its greatest indictment.

The school cook was unkind as well as being unhygienic. She spoiled the food with her careless, filthy habits. Did the wealthy Rev Wilson hear of this? He most certainly did and 'his reply was to the effect that the children were to be trained up to regard higher things than dainty pampering of the appetite and (apparently, unconscious of the fact, that daily loathing and rejection of food is sure to undermine their health) he lectured them on the sin of caring over-much for carnal things.'[16] By November 1824 Emily had joined her sisters at Cowan Bridge.

If carelessness with food was not bad enough for the health of the girls, there was another death trap. Let Mrs Gaskell take up the story:

'There was another trial of health common to all the girls. The path from Cowan Bridge to Dunstall Church where Mr Wilson preached, and where they all attended on a Sunday, is more than two miles in length, and goes sweeping along the rise and fall of the unsheltered country, in a way to make it a fresh and exhilarating walk in summer, but a bitter cold one in winter, especially to children whose thin blood flowed languidly in consequence of their half-starved condition.

'The church was not warmed, there being no means for this purpose. It stands in the midst of fields, and the damp mists must have gathered round the walls and crept in at the windows. The girls took their cold dinner with them and ate it between the services, in a chamber over the entrance, opening out of the former galleries.

'The arrangements for this day were peculiarly trying to delicate children, particularly to those who were spiritless, and longing for home, as poor Maria Brontë must have been. For her, ill health was increasing; the old cough, the remains of the whooping-cough, lingered about her; she was far superior in mind to any of her play-fellows and companions, and was lonely amongst them from that very cause; and yet she had faults so annoying that she was in constant disgrace with her teachers, and an object of merciless dislike to one of them who is depicted as "Miss Scatcherd" in *Jane Eyre,* and whose real name I will be merciful enough not to disclose.

'I need hardly say that Helen Burns is as exact a transcript of Maria Brontë as Charlotte's wonderful power of reproducing character could give. Her heart, to the latest day on which we met, still beat with unavailing indignation at the worrying and the cruelty to which her gentle, patient, dying sister had been subjected by this woman.'[17]

Dying sister? Sadly, it was so. In December 1824, Maria began to show the signs of consumption but, unbelievably, her father was not told. The filthy food at the school and sitting in church with wet feet did not aid her condition in any way. Neither did the behaviour of 'Miss Scatcherd' who was, in fact, Miss Andrews, a teacher who had been temporarily superintendent of the school while the Brontë girls were at

Cowan Bridge until the appointment of a teacher called Miss Evans.[18]

Mrs Gaskell spells out the disgraceful and cruel treatment of Maria through the testimony of a fellow pupil covering Miss Andrews by Charlotte's fictional name:

'The dormitory in which Maria slept was a long room, holding a row of narrow little beds on each side, occupied by the pupils; and at the end of this dormitory there was a small bed-chamber opening out of it, appropriated to the use of Miss Scatcherd. Maria's bed stood nearest to the door of this room.

'One morning, after she had become so seriously unwell as to have had a blister applied to her side (the sore from which was not perfectly healed), when the getting-up bell was heard, poor Maria moaned out that she was so ill, so very ill, she wished she might stop in bed; and some of the girls urged her to do so, and said they would explain it all to Miss Temple, the superintendent. But Miss Scatcherd was close at hand, and her anger would have to be faced before Miss Temple's kind thoughtfulness could interfere; so the sick children began to dress, shivering with cold, as, without leaving her bed she slowly put on her black worsted stockings over her thin white legs (my informant spoke as if she saw it yet, and her whole face flashed out undying indignation).

'Just then Miss Scatcherd issued from her room, and, without asking for a word of explanation from the sick and frightened girl, she took her by the arm, on the side to which the blister had been applied, and by one vigorous movement whirled her out into the middle of the floor, abusing her all the time for dirty and untidy habits. There she left her. My informant says Maria hardly spoke, except to beg some of the more indignant girls to be calm; but, in slow, trembling movements, with many a pause, she went downstairs at last – and was punished for being late.'[19]

By February 1825, the condition of Maria's health had seriously deteriorated and her father was sent for. Mrs Gaskell points out that as he had not been previously aware of her illness, 'the condition in which he found her was a terrible shock to him. He took her home by the Leeds coach, the girls crowding out into the road to follow her with their eyes over the bridge, past the cottages, and then out of sight for ever.'[20]

Maria lived for just eleven more weeks, nursed by her father and her Aunt Elizabeth. What passed between them we will never know. She died on 6 May 1825 and was buried six days later in the vault beneath Haworth Church next to her mother.[21] It seems heartless to our twenty-first century sensibilities but Elizabeth, Charlotte and Emily remained at Cowan Bridge. Not for them to grieve at home with the comfort of loved ones.

Out of the furnace of it all, Charlotte became the carrier of Maria's flame to millions of her readers to this day. She made sure that the world will never forget her sister, 'a girl of fine imagination and extraordinary talents.' What could Maria not have written had she lived? The sad fact is that the conditions at her school in the nineteenth century were not all that rare.

The relentless hand of illness at Cowan Bridge did not lift in the weeks that followed. A type of typhus now broke out in the badly sanitised and dangerously fed school. The doctor recommended that the girls be sent to Silverdale on the Lancashire coast. It is a very pleasant cove with bracing winds coming off Morecambe Bay. The Rev Wilson had a holiday house there.[22] The ten-year-old Elizabeth Brontë did not leave with the rest of her fellow pupils for Silverdale. Now seriously ill, she was taken by a servant in the school, a Mrs Hardacre, by public coach to Keighley and by private gig to Haworth.[23] What were her thoughts as she neared home where her sister had so recently died?

As soon as Patrick saw Elizabeth's face he knew she had the fatal consumption. The very next day he set off for Silverdale and brought Elizabeth and Charlotte home.[24] He also removed them from the school, never to return. Can words be found to describe how the Brontë family, Patrick, Branwell, Anne, Charlotte, Emily and Miss Elizabeth Branwell felt as they all watched Elizabeth slip away from them? She died fifteen days after she had left Cowan Bridge with Mrs Hardacre. It all must have been horrendous. Out of all this mind-bending, heart-breaking sorrow three great writers would emerge. It is a truly extraordinary story that they ever did. Their emergence is now the fascinating subject of this book.

There is, obviously, a huge interest in what fed the imaginations of Patrick Brontë's children. We now know of the books the family owned from Oliver Goldsmith's *History of England* to Bunyan's *Pilgrim's Progress,* from Hannah More's *Moral Sketches* to Thomas Salmon's *New Geographical and Historical Grammar.* In the parsonage library the works of Homer and Horace, Milton, Walter Scott, Isaac Watts and Thomas à Kempis could be found and more.[25] Patrick's children knew the Scriptures thoroughly. Branwell was taught Latin by his father and it seems that the girls shared his lessons. From works by Charlotte, Emily and Anne we know they were familiar with classical language and literature. They also had access to books outside their home, particularly, it seems, from one of the circulating libraries at Keighley.[26]

It was, though, the monthly *Blackwood's Magazine* that put fire into the Brontë veins, founded in 1817 by the publisher William Blackwood. With its mixture of satire, review and criticism, it was extremely popular and quickly gained a large reading public. A Tory magazine, it, of course, covered politics, but through the years it also printed works by Shelley, Coldridge, Wordsworth, George Eliot, Joseph Conrad and James Hogg. It also horribly savaged the poetry of young John Keats. Aside from printing lots of essays, it also printed a good deal of horror fiction. It ceased publishing in 1980, having always remained in the ownership of the Blackwood family.

Taught art by John Bradley of the Keighley Mechanics Institute and music by the Haworth Parish organist, Abraham Sutherland, the Brontë children were surrounded by toys.[27] They gave their toys names and invented stories around them. With brimming and noisy enthusiasm they acted out their plays. Their early plays included, *The Young Men, Our Fellows,* and *The Islanders,* three plays which survive in written form today.

In the last of these, each child selected three heroes, which they chose from their knowledge of history, the military or politics, that they had learned about from their father or their reading. Also, each child became a 'genie' with the special power of being able to bring the dead back to life: this is often interpreted as wishful thoughts on their part for their dearly departed sisters and mother, whom they longed to have back.

The Young Men plays took rise from some wooden soldiers belonging to Branwell and *Our Fellows* from Aesop's Fables. From *The Young Men* plays the imaginary world of Glasstown emerged and, eventually, Angria.

The stories were written out in tiny books which the children made from scraps of paper. These were sown into covers made from the wrappings of parcels, bits of sugar bags and wallpaper. On each page, three to four hundred words were printed in microscopic size in italics. The reason for the minute size of this early writing is believed simply to be that it was meant to 'fit' or be proportional with the toy soldiers each of which could fit in the palms of their hands. We are, of course, talking of hundreds of thousands of words and the microscopic writing is said to have caused Charlotte's extreme short-sightedness.

Throughout this now famous juvenilia of the Brontës, the spelling is dreadful. Some of it is still in existence and is housed at the Brontë Parsonage Museum. All sorts of contemporary people were found in their stories. These included Sir James Clarke Ross and Sir William Edward Parry the Arctic explorer, who had been seeking to find a North West Passage and with whom the famous Banbridge man, Captain Francis Crozier, sailed on six outstanding expeditions to the ice. Other contemporary people in their stories included Napoleon Bonaparte, called Sneaky by Branwell, the Duke of York and, of course, Charlotte's favourite hero, the Duke of Wellington.

While all this juvenilia was flowing, Patrick lifted his pen in the *Leeds Intelligencer* in 1829 to bravely defend Roman Catholic Emancipation (albeit a limited emancipation).[28] Arguments on the subject, as already noted, raged around the fact that the Pope had the power to release his subjects from their obligation, even from an oath of loyalty to the State.

Patrick now defended the Roman Catholics right to vote, to sit in Parliament and to hold civic office provided they had the necessary property qualifications. He still held to his belief in the necessity for a Protestant Monarch or legislature to remove Catholics from 'all places of trust or influence' if danger threatened. In his more 'liberal' view he differed hugely with his evangelical contemporaries. For an Irish evangelical clergyman, to defend even this limited form of emancipation was a rare stance indeed. Patrick also continued his campaign to change the severity of the criminal code.[29]

In January 1829, Branwell launched *Branwell's Blackwood's Magazine* helped by Charlotte. It was 'issued' monthly, was 5.5 by 3.5 centimetres in size, and ran for two years. It was later renamed *Young Men's Magazine* by Charlotte, who became its editor when Branwell got bored with it. Branwell then produced a little newspaper called *Monthly Intelligencer*. He also wrote poetry and completed a verse play.

The picture emerges of a little family hard-pressed by recent sorrow and rising above it by entering the world of the imagination expressed in art and literature. They were outwardly protected by their loving father, desperately seeking to make ends meet financially, surrounded by a parish facing increasing unemployment and poverty and to which he conscientiously and continually ministered. He also helped organise petitions for the abolition of slavery and the revision and mitigation of the criminal code to the House of Commons and the House of Lords. Here was an extraordinary family, indeed.

The pressure of it all began to affect Patrick's health and he became seriously ill in 1830 with an inflammation of the lungs. Death, it seems, seriously threatened him.[30] The crisis, mercifully, passed, but Patrick, weakened and depressed, struggled on. Soon, though, he'd have to let Charlotte go. She was fourteen, needed formal qualifications for any future employment, and must return to school again. But where?

Six
Picking Up Gold

'I FIRST saw her coming out of a covered cart, in very old-fashioned clothes, and looking very cold and miserable. She was coming to school at Miss Wooler's. When she appeared in the schoolroom her dress was changed, but just as old. She looked a little old woman, so short-sighted that she always appeared to be seeking something, and moving her head from side to side to catch a sight of it. She was very shy and nervous and spoke with a strong Irish accent.'[1]

Such was fellow-pupil Mary Taylor's description of Charlotte Brontë on the day she arrived at the Clergy Daughters' School at Roe Head near Mirfield, within the West Riding of Yorkshire. It was a fine eighteenth century three-storey grey building with large and pleasant gardens well situated on a rising slope. Roe Head was about 20 miles from Haworth and was run by Miss

Margaret Wooler and her sisters, Eliza, Susan, Catherine and Marianne.

The contrast with Cowan Bridge could not have been starker. There were usually between seven and ten pupils at the school and it was by nature more like a private school. Here, food was good and plentiful, the building warm, cheerful and roomy, and the teachers were respected and not feared. The ravages of the persecuting discipline of Cowan Bridge's Miss Wilson were unknown. The headmistress became Charlotte's friend for life. Charlotte would one day be offered the position of headmistress of Roe Head and, though she did not take it, her relationship with Miss Wooler was the antithesis of that which Charlotte had with the Rev Carus Wilson.

Charlotte was desperately homesick in her first days at Roe Head in the new term of January 1831. Eight days into the term another new pupil arrived. Ellen Nussey, though she came from only five miles away, was also homesick. On arrival at the school, Ellen found the girls were just going out to play. She was ushered into a schoolroom and left alone to settle down. Feeling homesick and rather awestruck by her surroundings, Ellen was surprised to find a girl crouched by the bow-window of the schoolroom, looking out on the snow-mantled landscape, crying.

Ellen went forward and spoke to Charlotte, admitting her own homesickness. They stood weeping together but out of their shared homesickness came an amazing friendship.[2] From the spring holidays of May 1831 until Charlotte's death, Ellen Nussey kept every letter Charlotte Brontë wrote to her. There are now over four hundred of these letters available to read and they give us a deep insight into Charlotte's life and character.

From Ellen we learn of Charlotte's beautiful soft-silky brown hair then 'dry and frizzy looking, screwed up in little tight curls, showing features that were all the plainer from her exceeding thinness and want of complexion, she looked "dried in". A dark, rusty green stuff dress of old fashioned make detracted still from her appearance.'[3] Mary Taylor, who also became Charlotte's lifelong school friend, fearing it was 'not safe' to keep them, destroyed every letter she received from Charlotte.

From Ellen and Mary a portrait emerges of a Charlotte who, though first thought eccentric, was actually an extraordinary fourteen-year-old. Mary Taylor told Charlotte directly and cruelly that she was very ugly.[4] Yet here was a teenager who wrote poetry, produced skilful pencil drawings and watercolours, and who could invent stories and characters at the drop of a hat. Mary Taylor soon had to admit that Charlotte knew things 'out of our range altogether'.[5] Charlotte picked up every scrap of information about painting, sculpture, music and poetry, said Mary, as if they were gold.[6]

Charlotte's storytelling powers were formidable. One story about the wanderings of a sleepwalker had so powerful an effect on one girl that she was reduced to shivering with terror! Charlotte soon became the dormitory storyteller *extraordinaire* until she and her audience were fined by the headmistress for 'late-talking'![7] Here was English literature's future mistress of storytelling at work early in her career. Charlotte also picked up three prizes at the close of her first half-year and was awarded the silver medal for 'the fulfilment of duties' with the word 'Emulation' on the obverse side of the medal and the word 'Rewarded' on the other. Soon Charlotte was at the top of the school.

Determined to fulfil her aim of self-improvement, Mary Taylor tells us that 'she liked the stated task to be over, that she might be free to pursue her self-appointed ones ... when her companions were merry round the fire or otherwise engaging themselves during the twilight, which was always a precious time of relaxation, she would be kneeling close to the window busy with her studies, and this would last so long that she was accused of seeing in the dark.'[8]

Charlotte also began to be stretched socially as she was invited to her friends' houses at weekends or for short holidays. At the Red House in Gomersal, Charlotte found the Taylors a very different kettle of fish to her own Anglican family. A radical and dissenting family, Jonathan Taylor was a wool cloth manufacturer. Apart from Mary there was tomboy Martha, dour Calvinistic Mrs Taylor, and her four sons. They all argued, debated and discussed politics, religion and literature all day and every evening! Charlotte loved it, even vigorously defending her hero, the Duke of Wellington, in the midst of it all.

Charlotte's visits to The Rydings, the elegant, castillated old home with its large grounds and fine chestnut trees in Birstall were very different to those to the Red House. Described by Branwell, who walked there to see his sister Charlotte, as 'Paradise', it was home to a Church of England family who were deeply conservative.

Ellen Nussey was the youngest of twelve children. She had lost her father, John, a wool merchant, when she was nine years of age. The family now lived at The Rydings with her Uncle Richard. Life at The Rydings was all polite and refined and Charlotte was readily and courteously accepted amidst all the comings and goings of a large family, the oldest of whom was twenty years her senior.

Charlotte stayed at Roe Head, apart from summer and Christmas holidays at home, for eighteen months. She won the silver medal for achievement three times in succession and eventually left the school in June 1832. It had all been very successful. One of the greatest things to happen to her there was, of course, the wonderful friendship that emerged with Ellen Nussey which was to last for twenty-four years. Ellen was to remain to the end of her life the most outstanding defender of the name and honour of Charlotte Brontë. Today, biographers of the Brontës owe her a huge debt.

In a letter to W S Williams on 3 June 1850, Charlotte wrote: 'When I first saw Ellen I did not care for her; we were school fellows. In the course of time we learnt each other's faults and good points. We were contrasts – still we suited. Affection was a first germ, then a sapling, then a strong tree – now, no new friend however lofty or profound in intellect ... could be to me what Ellen is; yet she is no more than a conscientious, observant, calm, well-bred Yorkshire girl. She is without romance. If she attempts to read poetry or poetic prose aloud, I am irritated and deprive her of the book – if she talks of it, I stop my ears; but she is good; she is true; she is faithful and I love her.'[9]

Charlotte's family also grew to love Ellen. In July 1833, Ellen paid her first visit to Haworth to be followed by many others. Her description of the Haworth parsonage, recorded years later, gives to the modern reader a rare glimpse into the life of the Brontë family.

We learn of the fifty-six-year-old Patrick with his snow-white hair. We learn of his high white cravat which he covered by winding several wrappings of white sewing-silk. This huge eccentric cravat, visible in a photograph of him at the time, was worn to protect him from bronchial complaints. We learn of the clock halfway up the stairs which he wound up every night on his way to bed after family prayers. We learn of the animals in the home and the oatmeal porridge for breakfast. We also learn of the Rev Brontë's habit of sleeping with a loaded pistol closely available and of his discharging it from his bedroom window each morning. This was not, be it noted again, because of bad temper or displeasure. It was not, though, something Ellen was used to on mornings at The Rydings! Descriptions are given of Aunt Branwell, Tabby Aykroyd, 'the faithful trustworthy old servant' quaint in appearance.

From Ellen we learn that the Brontë children were all small of stature. Charlotte in full adulthood was only 4ft 9inches and Emily was the tallest at 5ft 3inches. We learn of the fifteen-year-old Emily having a 'lithesome, graceful figure' and having 'kind, kindling, liquid eyes'. 'Dear, gentle Anne' had 'beautiful, violet-blue eyes' and 'fine pencilled eyebrows' and a 'clear almost transparent complexion'. Her hair was a pretty light brown colour and 'fell on her neck in graceful curls'.

Ellen writes nothing of Branwell except that he studied regularly with his father, painted in oils and that all the family hoped he would one day be a professional and distinguished artist.[10] Early in 1833, Branwell had already decided he would become a portrait painter. We learn, from other sources, that though small for his age, he was good-looking, had his father's aquiline nose, high forehead and red hair. He also had poor eyesight. He was excitable, emotional and unable to conceal his feelings.[11]

The next three years at the Brontë parsonage show the Brontë family hard at work on their stories and poems of the imaginary world of Angria and Gondal. All kinds of themes rise in this juvenilia including rebellion, questions about Christian teaching, religious hypocrisy and cant. Other themes included Yorkshire dialect, magic, omens and mysterious strangers. Patrick made no attempt to discourage his children's writing, though 'he did encourage them to channel their energies into less secret projects.'[12]

He presented Charlotte at Christmas 1833 with a manuscript notebook in which he had written on the top of the first page: '1833. All that is written in this book must be in good, plain and legible hand.'[13] He was, obviously, anxiously seeking to draw Charlotte away from the minute cramped handwriting that had given her such chronic short-sightedness. He also bought a cottage piano to encourage his children's musical talents. Charlotte was into watercolour portraits at this time having at one time 'had the notion of making her living as an artist.'[14]

The most famous portrait of the three Brontë sisters by Branwell, which now hangs in the National Portrait Gallery in London, emerged in 1834. The portrait that was described by Mrs Gaskell as 'good likenesses, however badly executed'[15] is now, ironically, one of the most popular in the National Portrait Gallery. Branwell included himself in the portrait and then immediately painted himself out again. As the years pass the badly-mixed paint has become transparent and the ghostly image of Branwell is re-emerging.

All the Brontës took turns to become Sunday School teachers, their father having worked hard to have a new Sunday School building erected. He also successfully campaigned for a Temperance Society in Haworth and was appointed its President.

Things, though, in life, do not remain the same for very long. On 2 July 1835, Charlotte wrote to Ellen Nussey: 'We're all about to divide, break-up, separate, Emily is going to school, Branwell is going to London, and I am going to be a governess. This last determination I have formed myself, knowing that I should have to take this step sometime, and "better ... as syne" to use the Scotch proverb and knowing also that Papa would have enough to do with his limited income should Branwell be placed at the Royal Academy, and Emily at Roe Head.'[16]

Miss Wooler had offered Charlotte a post as a teacher at Roe Head agreeing that part of her salary would pay for Emily's board and tuition. As it turned out, Charlotte's time as a teacher at Roe Head turned out to be most unhappy. Emily's experience proved to be no better than Charlotte's. In truth, Charlotte did not like the children under her care and detested the fact that she now had so little privacy with precious little time at her disposal. It all led to a crisis. Any odd time she had she would steal away into the fantasy world of Angria, daydreaming and writing about it. There now emerged a real conflict between her Christian faith and her imagination. Her father was urging her to concentrate more closely to her duties and to watch her obsession with the world of the imagination which was threatening to interfere with the real world.

There is an incredible description Charlotte gives of one of her flights of imagination as she sat in the dining room one evening at Roe Head and how 'this foot trod the war-shaken shores of the Calabar and these light eyes saw the defiled and violated Adrianopolis shedding its lights on the river from lattices whence the invader looked out and was not darkened; ... while this apparition was before me the dining room door opened and Miss Wooler came in with a plate of butter in her hand. "A very stormy night, my dear!" said she. "It is ma'am," said I.'[17]

Phyllis Bentley sums up the tension very well. She writes of how Ellen Nussey's letters 'urged religious consolations upon her' and of how 'Charlotte struggled to bow her head and adopt these.'[18] Charlotte wrote to Ellen declaring: 'My darling, if I were like you, I should have my face Zionward, though prejudice and error might occasionally fling a mist over the glorious vision before me, but *I am not like you.* If you knew my thoughts, the dreams that absorb me, and fiery imagination that at times eats me up, and makes me feel society, as it is, wretchedly insipid, you would pity and I dare say despise me. But I know the treasures of the *Bible*; I love and adore them. I can *see* the Well of Life in all its clearness and brightness, but when I stoop down to drink of the pure waters they fly from my lips as if I were Tantalus.'[18]

Ellen could have had no idea of the depth of those firey imaginations. Only a few days before the date of Charlotte's letter to Ellen, she was writing a story in which she was torn between 'her sincere moral beliefs and her powerful urge to write of illicit amours.'[20] Phyllis Bentley comments: 'Her characterisation in this story is really splendid; this girl of barely twenty from a remote country parsonage displays the difference between the pale Duchess of Zamorna in her quiet dress and Mina in black satin and ruby ear-rings, both women made equally unhappy by the man they love, with a skill greater and more subtle than that, say, of Ouida. Anyone who has daydreamed in spheres their normal beliefs forbid – and this is the essential nature of a Freudian daydream – and tried to break the habit will know the keen agony of the effort, and glorious relief of its abandonment.'[21]

Charlotte was, without doubt, having a spiritual crisis. 'I have strings of conscience,' she wrote to Ellen, 'visitings of remorse, glimpses of holy, of inexpressible things, which formerly I used to be a stranger to; it may all die away, and I may be in utter midnight, but I implore a merciful Redeemer, that, if this be the dawn of the gospel, it may still brighten to perfect day ... I am in that state of horrid, gloomy uncertainty that, at this moment, I would submit to be old, grey-haired, to have passed all my youthful days of enjoyment, and to be settling on the verge of the grave, if I could only thereby ensure the prospect of reconciliation with God, and redemption through his Son's merits.'[22]

At this time Charlotte wrote to the poet Southey, sending him some of her poetry and asking his opinion. He replied warning her of the dangers of daydreams and, typical of his times, told her that 'literature cannot be the business of a woman's life, and it ought not to be!' He urged upon her 'proper duties' and to write poetry for poetry's sake.[23]

Southey little knew that Charlotte's gift was to far outstrip his own and that her future novels would straddle the ages. No wonder she became the incredible feminist she became, though, in the immediate, she wrote back to him thanking him for the advice and trusted that she would never 'more feel ambitious to see my name in print; if the wish should arise, I'll look at Southey's letter and suppress it.'[24]

Charlotte's spiritual crisis continued and she wrote of her 'evil wandering thoughts, my corrupt heart, cold to the spirit, and warm to the flesh.' She wanted to 'become better, far better' and wrote of longing for holiness 'which I shall, never, never obtain.'[25] She was in truth trying to work her way to salvation while at the same time worried that she was not predestined to salvation in the first place. It was not what her father preached for he espoused the doctrine of repentance toward God and faith in Jesus Christ as the sole means of salvation available to all.

Fascinatingly, Anne Brontë now plunged into a similar crisis of doubting the prospect of her own salvation. Anne fell seriously ill with gastric fever and the Rev James de la Trobe, who visited her several times during her illness, wrote of 'her life being on a slender thread'.[26] Charlotte, deeply concerned about Anne's state of health, approached Miss Wooler who decried it by saying Anne only had a common cold. A serious tiff arose with Charlotte resolving to leave the school when Miss Wooler wisely initiated reconciliation.

Who then was the Rev James de la Trobe? He was, interestingly, a Moravian minister and teacher of the Moravian

Chapel and School in Mirfield. Here was an antidote for Anne's misery of soul and body if ever there was one. Perhaps William Wilberforce, who was influenced by Moravians, best summed up the attitude and ethos of this very special group of people. This 'body of Christians,' wrote Wilberforce, 'have perhaps excelled all mankind in solid and unequivocal proofs of the love of Christ, and of the most ardent and active and patient zeal in his service. It is a zeal tempered with prudence, softened with meekness, soberly aiming at great ends by the gradual operation of well-adapted means, supported by a courage which no danger can intimidate, and a quiet constancy which no hardship can exhaust.'[27]

Moravians are particularly associated with the great Christian leader, Count Zinzendorf, who wrote the famous hymn, *Jesus, Thy Blood and Righteousness*. Its words beautifully sum up the doctrine held by the Moravian minister who visited Anne Brontë in her time of spiritual crisis:

Jesus, Thy blood and righteousness
My beauty are, my glorious dress;
'Midst flaming worlds, in these arrayed,
With joy shall I lift up my head.

Bold shall I stand in that great day,
For who aught to my charge shall lay?
Fully absolved through these I am,
From sin and fear, from guilt and shame.

When from the dust of death I rise
To claim my mansion in the skies;
E'en then shall this be all my plea,
'Jesus hath lived and died, for me.'

This spotless robe the same appears,
When ruined nature sinks in years;
No age can change its glorious hue,
The robe of Christ is ever new.

Jesus, the endless praise to Thee,
Whose boundless mercy hath for me -
For me a full atonement made,
An everlasting ransom paid.

O, let the dead now hear Thy voice,
Bid, Lord, Thy banished ones rejoice;
Their beauty this, their glorious dress,
Jesus, the Lord our Righteousness![28]

From the Rev de la Trobe we learn that Anne at this time turned away from trying to keep God's law to earn her salvation to accepting salvation as God's gift to her in Christ and so finding comfort and peace.

Let de la Trobe's words sum up her experience: 'I found her well acquainted with the main truths of the Bible respecting our salvation, but seeing them more through the law than the gospel, more as a requirement from God than his gift in his Son, but her heart opened to the sweet views of salvation, pardon, and peace in the blood of Christ, and she accepted his welcome to the weary and heavy-ladened sinner, conscious more of her not loving the Lord her God than of acts of enmity to him, and, had she died then, I should have counted her his redeemed and ransomed child.'[29]

Anne now left Roe Head School for good and returned to the congeniality of home and quickly recovered her health. What, though, of Charlotte and Angora?

SEVEN

Spitting into a Workbag

BY JANUARY 1839 things had moved on for the Brontë family. Branwell had not gone to study at the Royal Academy in London but had now taken a studio in Bradford as a professional portrait painter. He had taken lodgings with a beer dealer at No. 2 Fountain Street. By now he was a Master Mason at the Haworth Masonic Lodge.

As for Emily, she had taken a teaching post at a girl's school at Law Hill on the outskirts of Halifax. It was a large school of nearly forty pupils and she was hard at work from 6.00am until nearly 11.00 at night with only half-an-hour for exercise between. She had turned to poetry in particular for solace; it was marked for its attempt to capture the beauty of the Yorkshire moorland.

For the moors, for the moors, where the short grass
Like velvet beneath us should lie!
For the moors, for the moors, where each high pass
Rose sunny against the clear sky!

For the moors, where the linnet was trilling
Its song on the old granite stone.
Where the lark – the wild – lark was filling
Every breast with delight like its own.[1]

Anne was still at home in Haworth with her father. Patrick had survived very difficult and acrimonious times with the Dissenters of Haworth over a campaign regarding the vexed question of their having to pay church rates for the Established Anglican Church to which they did not belong. Patrick had opposed them tooth and nail. He had also vigorously and publicly campaigned against the repeal of the Poor Law Amendment Act which was causing serious hardship in Yorkshire. He, one of the founder members of the Haworth Temperance Society, was now taking a daily glass of wine with his main meal for 'his stomach's sake.' It had been recommended by a young Keighley surgeon for his dyspepsia.[2]

As for Charlotte, she had come out of what was for her a real nightmare. She had asked of her school teaching career in August 1836: 'The thought came over me, am I to spend the best part of my life in this wretched bondage, forcibly surpressing my rage at the whims, the apathy and the hyperbolical and most assinine stupidity of these fat-headed oafs and on completion assuming an air of kindness, patience and acidity?'[3]

Roe Head School had been moved to Heald's House at Dewsbury Moor some three to four miles away due to changing circumstances in Miss Wooler's family. Depressed, isolated, overwrought, impatient with her pupils, deeply frustrated that she had precious little time to write, subject to morbid thoughts, Charlotte finally cut loose and returned home to Haworth. Her doctor had told her to go home if she valued her life. We, her readers, owe that doctor a great debt.[4]

Charlotte's equilibrium returned as she could now re-immerse herself in her writing. Now, ever so slowly, the portents of her greatest creation, *Jane Eyre*, emerged in one of her Angrian stories. Her character Elizabeth Hastings has many of her own and Jane's characteristics. Elizabeth refuses to become Sir William Percy's mistress in much the same manner and for similar reasons as Jane was to refuse Mr Rochester.[5] The butterfly was slowly beginning to form in the seemingly inactive chrysalis.

At the very same time as Charlotte was writing her story of Elizabeth Hastings and Sir William Percy, in March 1839 she received without any previous hint whatsoever, a proposal of marriage. It came from Ellen's brother, the Rev Henry Nussey, a former curate at Dewsbury, now in a new curacy at Donnington in Suffolk. If Charlotte had been looking for an escape route to financial security, here was an obvious one to take. Henry was an amiable, eligible, conscientious clergyman four years her senior. Charlotte, though, had one overiding reason for refusing him. She, unlike many Victorian women in her century, was determined to marry for love. She did not love Henry and, in a diplomatically superb letter, turned him down without a word of sarcasm or annoyance.[6] Not a nuance in the letter was designed to hurt him in any way.

Henry Nussey foreshadows the Rev St John Rivers in *Jane Eyre* at lots of levels. His cold, dismissive, passionless entry in his diary on the 9 March 1839, says it all: 'Received an unfavourable reply from Charlotte Brontë. The will of the Lord be done.'[7]

Meanwhile, Branwell decided to give up his studio in Bradford and return home. He was in a hugely competitive field of work and was not making enough money to give him any prospect of a secure future. Hot on his heels came Emily, broken in health, returning home for good from Law Hill.

Patrick, now sixty-two years of age, had his four children under his roof again, all unemployed. It was, interestingly, the gentle, quiet Anne who now decided to venture outside her extraordinary family to take up employment as a governess with the Ingham family at Blake Hall, near Mirfield. It was a formidable day for the nineteen-year-old as she set out alone, by her own choice, to Mirfield. Determined to prove that she was capable, she soon experienced a baptism of fire.

The Ingham children were uncontrollable and verbally and physically abused their governess. Anne received no support from Mr and Mrs Ingham in her attempts to discipline their children. She soon discovered the contempt and downright inhumanity that was often shown towards the poor though educated women of the Victorian age, whose only resource was to become a governess. Little did the Ingham's know it, but the quiet Anne would one day lift her pen and expose the cruel snobbery she experienced at Blake Hall in her novel *Agnes Grey*. An incident in the story proves this truth:

'I particularly remember one wild, snowy afternoon, soon after my return in January; the children had all come up from dinner, loudly declaring that they meant "to be naughty"; and they had well kept their resolution, though I had talked myself hoarse, and wearied every muscle in my throat, in the vain attempt to reason them out of it. I had got Tom pinned up in a corner, whence, I told him, he should not escape till he had done his appointed task. Meantime, Fanny had possessed herself of my workbag, and was rifling its contents, and spitting into it besides. I told her to let it alone, but to no purpose, of course.

"'Burn it, Fanny!" cried Tom; and *this* command she hastened to obey. I sprang to snatch it from the fire, and Tom darted to the door.

"'Mary Ann, throw her desk out of the window!" cried he; and my precious desk, containing my letters and papers, my small amount of cash, and all my valuables was about to be precipitated from the three-storey window. I flew to rescue it. Meanwhile, Tom had left the room, and was rushing down the stairs, followed by Fanny. Having secured my desk, I ran to catch them, and Mary Ann came scampering after. All three escaped me, and ran out of the house into the garden, where they plunged about in the snow, shouting and screaming in exultant glee.

'What must I do? If I followed them, I should probably be unable to capture one, and only drive them farther away; if I did not, how was I to get them in? And what would their parents think of me, if they saw or heard the children rioting, hatless, bonnetless, gloveless, and bootless, in the deep, soft snow?

'While I stood in this perplexity, just without the door, trying by grim looks and angry words to awe them into subjection, I heard a voice behind me, in harshly piercing tones, exclaiming, "Miss Grey! Is it possible? What, in the devil's name, can you be thinking about?"

"'I can't get them in, Sir," said I, turning round, and beholding Mr Bloomfield, with his hair on end and his pale blue eyes bolting from their sockets.

"'But I *insist* upon their being got in!" cried he, approaching nearer, and looking perfectly ferocious.

"'Then, Sir, you must call them yourself, if you please, for they won't listen to me," I replied, stepping back.

"'Come in with you, you filthy brats! or I'll horsewhip you, every one!" roared he; and the children instantly obeyed. "There, you see! They come at the first word!"

"'Yes, when *you* speak."

"'And it's very strange, that when you've the care of 'em, you've no better control over 'em than that? Now, there they are, gone upstairs with their nasty snowy feet! Do go after 'em and see them made decent, for heaven's sake!"

'That gentleman's mother was then staying in the house; and, as I ascended the stairs and passed the drawing-room door, I had the satisfaction of hearing the old lady declaiming aloud to her daughter-in-law to this effect (for I could only distinguish the most emphatic words), "Gracious Heavens! – never in all my life! – ! – get their death as sure as – ! Do you think, my dear, she's a *proper person*? Take my word for it – "'[8]

One might be tempted to think that Anne was exaggerating with her description of such an incident. Let it be noted, though, that a descendant of the Inghams later told the story of an actual incident that bears strong resemblance to the incident described in *Agnes Grey*.[9]

Anne, in recent literary history, has often been presented as 'the forgotten Brontë'. Charlotte had adopted a 'motherly', protective attitude to Anne following the death of her mother and her sisters, Maria and Elizabeth. She really did not have a deep confidence in her as a writer. In her biographical notice in 1850, rectifying the general perception that all works published under the names of Currer, Ellis and Acton Bell were the production of one person, namely herself, Charlotte wrote of Anne:

'Anne's character was milder and more subdued; she wanted the power, the fire, the originality of her sister, but was well endowed with quiet virtues of her own. Long-suffering, self-denying, reflective and intelligent, a constitutional reserve and taciturnity placed and kept her in the shade, and covered her mind, and especially her feelings, with a sort of nun-like veil, which was rarely lifted. Neither Emily nor Anne was learned; they had no thought of filling their pitchers at the wellspring of other minds; they always wrote from the impulse of nature, the dictates of intuition, and from such stores of observation as their limited experience had enabled them to amass. I may sum up all by saying that for strangers they were nothing; but for those who had known them all their lives in the intimacy of close relationship, they were genuinely good and truly great.'[10]

Those of us, once strangers to the writing of Anne Brontë, through reading her exposure of widespread upper-class behaviour as seen through the eyes of a humble and materially poor governess, have come to see that she was a very distinguished writer. She was one who, in the words of Agnes Grey, endeavoured 'to live to the glory of him who has scattered so many blessings in our path.'[11]

Recent republishing of her works and recent reassessment of their value have resulted in her work becoming increasingly more appreciated. Anne had more fire running in her veins than was first realised. Charlotte felt it was her sacred duty to Anne and Emily 'to wipe the dust of their gravestones, and leave their dear names free from soil.'[12] The filtering power of history is now doing that work even more effectively for Anne.

Charlotte, now stirred to action, accepted a post as a governess with the Sidgwick family. They lived in the winter months in the gatehouse at Skipton Castle and in the summer at Stonegappe near the village of Lothersdale, about twelve miles from Haworth. Stonegappe was set in beautiful countryside high on a hill overlooking the flood valley of the River Aire.

Like Anne, Charlotte found her charges uncontrollable. Indeed, Charlotte was hit a severe blow on the temple by a stone thrown by her pupil, John, egged on by his older brother.[13] The snobbish Mrs Sidgwick looked down on Charlotte and their two personalities clashed, often. The appointment was not permanent, much to Charlotte's relief, and lasted only from May to July 1839.

Charlotte's employers may not have thought much of her but a young Irish clergyman did. The Rev David Pryce stayed at the Haworth parsonage for a few days that summer with Patrick's new curate, the Rev William Hodson. He was, in fact, Hodson's own curate and he fell in love with Charlotte at first sight. Fresh from Dublin University, he was a congenial, witty and intelligent young man. He proposed to Charlotte by letter a few days later. She turned him down. Within less than six months, David Pryce died very suddenly. Charlotte was to discover, as do all of us, that life is much stranger than fiction.

In the summer of 1839, Charlotte got her first glimpse of the sea while on holiday. Like many writers before and after she was to carry a deep love of the various moods and seasons of the sea.

That autumn Emily was immersed in writing her poetry. Tabby Akroyd, the long-time servant of the Brontë household, now moved into retirement and Anne arrived home for the Christmas holidays. Anne had been dismissed by the Ingham family who, on finding no visible improvement in their children, blamed Anne. Unknown to them, the young woman disappearing over the hills from Blake Hall would bring millions of readers back to haunt their legacy of arrogance when she would write her novel *Agnes Grey*.

The year 1840 saw Branwell become a tutor to two boys, John and William Postlethwaite in Broughton-in-Furness in the

Lake District. He took the opportunity of sending one of his poems to Hartley Coleridge, eldest son of the great poet Samuel Taylor Coleridge.[14]   He also included two translations of Horace's *Odes*.[15] Much to Branwell's delight, Coleridge replied to his letter. Branwell, with Brontë fire in his veins, went over to Rydal Water and spent a day with Coleridge.[16]   Literary promise was now feeding his imagination.

Branwell was the Brontë who seemed to promise so much in the world of the arts in his family. To whom much is given, though, is much expected and Branwell, sadly, did not live up to what was expected of him. Two months later he was dismissed from the employment of William Postlethwaite because, it seems, he fathered a child by one of the daughters of the servants at Broughton House. The child, according to one source that we know about, died.[17] Branwell's poem, *Epistle from a Father on Earth to his Child in her Grave* written in 1846, seems to be autobiographical.[18]

Branwell was increasingly proving that he was very much the chameleon, able to suit the circumstances he was in, be it in a raucous drinking bar or an Anglican rector's home. It is acknowledged that he was seriously led astray by friendship with one William Brown, brother of the sexton of Haworth Church. Branwell had real talent as a writer and this was acknowledged by Coleridge and can be clearly seen today, particularly in his poetry. Eventually he was appointed a clerk with the new Leeds-Manchester Railway at Sowerby Bridge near Halifax.

The year 1841 brought a very significant decision on the part of Charlotte and Emily. Charlotte was now employed as a governess with the White family of Upperwood House at Rawdon in West Yorkshire; she was still struggling with the whole scene of teaching as a governess under the employ of families. The three Brontë girls, led by Charlotte, now began to think of running their own school. The independence this would bring was a huge attraction both from a financial point of view and in the prospect of having a school completely under their control. Their Aunt Branwell offered a loan to help get the school established.

Interestingly, at this time, Miss Elizabeth Wooler offered Charlotte the opportunity of taking over her school as headmistress. It was a truly attractive offer and Charlotte was tempted to accept. However, another temptation began to take root in her heart and mind. Her friend Mary Taylor had gone to Brussels with her sister Martha and they were enrolled at a school in the Château de Koekelberg. Mary's correspondence with Charlotte had quickened the fire in her veins for foreign travel.

Commenting on one of Mary's letters, Charlotte wrote to Ellen on 7 August 1841: 'I hardly know what swelled to my throat as I read her letter: such a vehement impatience of restraint and steady work; such a strong wish for wings – wings such as wealth can furnish: such an urgent thirst to see, to know, to learn; something internal seemed to expand bodily for a minute. I was tantalised by the consciousness of faculties unexercised, then all collapsed, and I despaired.'[19] Her friends, though, encouraged her to spend some time at a foreign school in preparation for setting up her own. With her imagination fired by Mary Taylor's description of the art and cathedrals she had seen in Europe, Charlotte determined to go to Brussels to study and to take Emily with her.

Charlotte's determination to go to Brussels was to have an incalculable influence on her future as a writer. Her Aunt Branwell provided the funding and, having given her notice to the White family, Charlotte arrived home on Christmas Eve

1841. It was a time of busy preparation over the following weeks as she and Emily began packing for Brussels.

On 8 February 1842 they set out for the Continent in the company of their father who again showed his love and care for his daughters in determining to travel with them to Brussels to see them settled in. They were joined by Mary Taylor and her brother Joe who, by now, knew the journey well.

On arrival in London, the party stayed at a hotel known as the Chapter Coffee House on Paternoster Row. With three days at their disposal before catching the Ostend Packet at London Bridge Wharf, Charlotte was determined to see as much of the culture of the city as she possibly could.

Later it was all encapsulated in Charlotte's novel *Villette* when Lucy Snowe describes her feelings on awakening in London: 'The next day was the First of March, and when I awoke, rose and opened my curtain, I saw the risen sun struggling through fog. Above my head, above the housetops, co-elevate almost with the clouds, I saw a solemn, orbed mass, dark blue and dim – THE DOME. While I looked, my inner self moved: my spirit shook its always-fettered wings half loose; I had a sudden feeling as if I, who never yet truly lived, were at last about to taste life. In that morning my soul grew as fast as Jonah's gourd.

"'I did well to come," I said, proceeding to dress with speed and care. "I like the spirit of this great London which I feel around me. Who but a coward would pass his whole life in hamlets, and forever abandon his faculties to the eating rust of obscurity?"'[20]

Forty years previously Wordsworth had tried to capture his feelings about London on the morning of 2 September 1802 on Westminster Bridge:

Earth has not anything to show more fair:
Dull would he be of soul who could pass by
A sight so touching in its majesty:
This City now doth like a garment wear
The beauty of the morning; silent, bare,
Ships, towers, domes, theatres, and temples lie
Open unto the fields, and to the sky;
All bright and glittering in the smokeless air.
Never did sun more beautifully steep
In his first splendour valley, rock or hill;
Ne'er saw I, never felt, a calm so deep!
The river glideth at his own sweet will:
Dear God! The very houses seem asleep;
And all that mighty heart is lying still![21]

We can visualise Emily and Charlotte's eyes and hearts drinking in the full detail of the magnificent Westminster Abbey and the British Museum. We can also imagine the discussions between them as they viewed the pictures hanging in the National Gallery where they simply could not have imagined that their portraits would one day be displayed.

The party caught the Ostend Packet on Saturday 12 February and, on arriving on the Continent, proceeded for Brussels. The Pensionat Heger was in the Rue d'Isabelle in the centre of the city. The long, low two-storey building gave no indication of the beautiful garden within its walls. One side of the garden was overlooked by the Athénéé Royal, a boys' school. On one side of the garden ran a narrow walk known as the Allée défendue. This was out of bounds to the girl pupils of the Pensionnat Heger. Trees and shrubs with thick, dense foliage grew over this alleyway which was to play an important part in Charlotte's novels, *Villette* and *The Professor,* set in Brussels. The school was headed by the thirty-three-year-old Constantin Georges

Romain Heger and his wife Claire Zoë Heger who lived on the premises with their three small daughters.

Placing his daughters in the care of this friendly couple, Patrick then stayed with English friends who had recommended the school and made a very special visit to the battlefield at Waterloo.[22] It is hard for a twenty-first century world to fully understand how important this battle was in the life and imagination of the people of the nineteenth century, never to speak of the Brontës, particularly Patrick and Charlotte.

Thirty-two years previous to Patrick's visit to Waterloo, the Duke of Wellington had famously attended the Duchess of Richmond's ball in a coach builder's large workshop in the Rue de la Blanchisserie in Brussels on the eve of the battle. Napoleon Bonaparte, having broken the hinge between Wellington and the Prussians, was making straight for Brussels. Wellington was seeking to 'preserve calm in the city, and a sudden cancellation of the ball or the disappearance of many of his leading guests would give precisely the wrong impression.'[23] By two o'clock in the morning he had the firmest indication yet that Napoleon Bonaparte had broken the hinge between his army and that of the Prussians and was making straight for Brussels.[24]

As Patrick headed out of Brussels three decades later to try to capture the atmosphere of Waterloo, it is worth reflecting on Wellington's ride back along the Brussels road to his headquarters after the battle. He had, as noted in an earlier chapter, lost around 15,000 men dead and wounded, his Prussian ally General Blücher had lost around 7,000 and Napoleon 25,000. Wellington was 'sombre and dejected ... the few individuals who attended him wore, too, rather the aspect of a little funeral train rather than that of victors in one of the most important battles ever fought.'[25]

Eventually, Wellington ate his supper 'at a table laid for too many who would never dine again, looking up anxiously every time the door opened. He drank a single glass of wine, toasting the 'Memory of the Peninsular War.' Then 'he held up both his hands in an imploring attitude,' and said, "The hand of Almighty God has been upon me this day," lay down on a pallet on the floor and slept in an instant.'[26]

Wellington's doctor later approached him with the preliminary casualty list: 'As I entered, he sat up, his face covered with the dust and sweat of the previous day, and extended his hand to me, which I took and held in mine, whilst I told him of Gordon's death, and of such of the casualties as had come to my knowledge. He was much affected. I felt the tears dropping fast upon my hand. And looking towards him, saw them chasing one another in furrows over his dusty cheeks. He brushed them away suddenly with his left hand, and said to me in a voice tremulous with emotion, "Well, thank God, I don't know what it is to lose a battle; but certainly nothing can be more painful than to gain one with the loss of so many of one's friends."'[27]

Wellington always maintained that the battle was 'a close-run thing'. Lady Shelley later recalled how that with glistening eye and broken voice he spoke to her of the battle: "'I hope to God," he said one day, "that I have fought my last battle. It is a bad thing to be always fighting. While in the thick of it, I am much too occupied to feel anything; but it is wretched just after. It is quite impossible to think of glory. Both mind and feelings are exhausted. I am wretched even at the moment of victory, and I always say that next to a battle lost, the greatest misery is a battle gained. Not only do you lose those dear friends with whom you have been living, but you are forced to leave the wounded behind you. To be sure one tries to do the best for them, but how little that is! At such moments every feeling in your breast is deadened. I am now just beginning to retain my natural spirits, but I never wish for any more fighting.'"[28]

Patrick Brontë perhaps thought that day as he headed out of Brussels on the road to Waterloo that the last great battle had been fought on European soil. The horrendous truth was that in the century that followed him around 92 million people would die as a result of two World Wars. We are told that Patrick often spoke in his pulpit in later years of his recollections of the battlefield at Waterloo.[29] As he eventually left his daughters with the Hegers and travelled down through Flanders and Northern France he could not know that the future slaughter on Flanders fields would be represented by the blood red poppy that quietly grew in the countryside around him. Twenty million people were to die in the First World War, to be followed by around 72 million as a result of the Second.

Patrick's daughter, Emily, had one year previously written a poem entitled, *Shall earth no more inspire thee?* 'It,' says Juliet Barker, 'contained an important idea that was to recur in later poetry and also in *Wuthering Heights*: a longing for death that rejected conventional views of Heaven in favour of a Paradise that was as like earth as possible.'[30]

Catherine's dream in *Wuthering Heights* forced her to say to Nelly Dean: 'If I were in Heaven, Nelly, I should be extremely miserable.' She says: 'I dreamt, once, that I was there ... Heaven did not seem to be my home; and I broke my heart weeping to come back to earth; and the angels were so angry that they flung me out, into the middle of the heath on the top of Wuthering Heights; where I woke sobbing for joy.'[31]

Patrick, though, held to a much more inspiring and biblical truth. At the heart of his evangelical faith lay the truth of a future new earth. Why, of course, would the Scriptures call it 'a new earth' if it did not have something of the old earth in it? The Scriptures teach that this earth will eventually burn up.[31] Something may burn up, of course, but its atoms remain. The clear message of the Scriptures is that divine redemption not only redeems the body of the believer but it will also redeem the earth.[32] There was more going on at Calvary than just opening a way for our souls to be redeemed.

Patrick carried a message that would outlive the battles and conflicts of every century and point to a day when as Isaiah, one of Charlotte Brontë's favourite writers, prophesied: 'The wolf will live with the lamb, the leopard will lie down with the goat, the calf and the lion and the yearling together; and a little child will lead them. The cow will feed with the bear, their young will lie down together; and the lion will eat straw like the ox. The infant will play near the hole of the cobra, and the young child put his hand into the viper's nest. They will neither harm nor destroy on all my holy mountain, for all the earth will be full of the knowledge of the Lord as the waters cover the sea.'[33]

Another kind of battle, though, was going to erupt at the Pensionnat Heger back in Brussels as Patrick's two daughters tried to settle to study. The tenets of Roman Catholicism were going to clash with the two rector's daughters from Haworth with huge literary and spiritual repercussions. Another battle just as deep would also ensue, this time for the very heart and love of Charlotte Brontë.

EIGHT

Of Confession, Forbidden Love and Scandal

'IF THE national character of the Belgians is to be measured by the character of most of the girls in this school,' Charlotte Brontë wrote to Ellen Nussey in July 1842, 'it is a character scrupulously cold, selfish, animal and inferior; they are, besides, very mutinous and difficult for the teachers to manage and their principles are rotten to the core. We avoid them, which is not difficult to do, as we have the brand of Protestantism and Anglicism upon us.'[1] The girls in turn 'thought the new English pupils wild and scared looking, with strange, odd, insular ideas about dress.'[2]

If Charlotte did not have a high view of the Belgian girls in her school, she did not have a high view of the Roman Catholicism around her, either. The school was predominantly

Roman Catholic and, in the same letter of July 1842, she comments: 'People talk of the danger which Protestants expose themselves to in going to reside in Catholic countries and thereby running the chance of changing their faith. My advice to all Protestants who are tempted to do anything so besotted as turn Catholic is to walk over the sea to the Continent; to attend mass sedulously for a time; to note well the mummeries thereof; also the idiotic, mercenary aspect of all priests; and *then*, if they are still disposed to consider Papistry in any other light than a most feeble, childish piece of humbug, let them turn Papists at once – that's all. I consider Methodism, Quakerism, and the extremes of High and Low Churchism foolish, but Roman Catholicism beats them all. At the same time, allow me to tell you, that there are some Catholics who are as good as any Christians can be to whom the Bible is a sealed book, and much better than many Protestants.'

This was the Charlotte who was about to fall deeply in love with a Roman Catholic and to confess in a confessional box to a Roman Catholic priest!

Charlotte and Emily made very few friends, were very much 'the outsiders', and rarely engaged in conversation with others. Lessons were taught exclusively in French in which neither of the Brontë sisters were yet fluent. Emily did not like the Hegers though M Heger recognised, it seems, Emily's 'genius' as being higher than Charlotte's. He laid much store by her reasoning powers. As it turned out, his teaching methods were to have a profound effect particularly upon Charlotte's writing.

Charlotte took a very strong Protestant stance even in the essays she wrote for her Roman Catholic teacher. He did not, in any way, oppose her. He rigorously trained his pupils by reading and analysing passages from classical French authors; he then instructed them to develop essays, modeled on the style of the author in question, on a topic set by him or them. He then wrote detailed comments and suggestions in the wide margin of their essays which the pupils were to incorporate in a revised edition of the essays which they had produced.[3] The result? Emily detested the teaching system, but Charlotte submitted to it and it set her free from the excessively ornate literature style of her Angrian writings.

Heger relentlessly paired away unnecessary verbiage. He disciplined Charlotte's pen, taught her to control her ever-overflowing imagination. M Heger cared about every nuance, every phrase. He wrote at the end of one of her essays, '... how very much importance you must give to your details as you unfold your subject! You must sacrifice, without pity, everything that does not constitute to clarity, verisimilitude and effect.'[4] Within four years the world would begin to appreciate Charlotte's exquisite application of the accuracy of M Heger's advice. Charlotte got M Heger's advice and the world got *Jane Eyre*.

Charlotte and Emily were offered free board and lodging for another six months before their planned six months stay came to an end. This was in return for Charlotte teaching English and Emily teaching music. This continued until the autumn of 1842 when, as was a constant pattern in the life story of the Brontës, death raised its ugly head once more.

In August the twenty-eight-year-old Rev William Weightman, who had been Patrick Brontë's curate for the last three years, took cholera. It was a painful, lingering death and later Patrick reported: 'I generally visited him twice a day, joined with him in prayer, heard his request for the prayers of this congregation, listened to him whilst he expressed his entire dependence on the merits of the Saviour, heard his pious admonitions to his attendants, and saw him in tranquillity close his eyes on this bustling, vain, selfish world; so that I may truly say, his end was peace, and his hope glory.'[5]

Much loved and deeply mourned by the people of Haworth, William Weightman had barely passed away when Mary Taylor's vivacious sister Martha died at the Château Koekelberg of cholera. Following tragically on the heels of these heart-breaking deaths came the death of Aunt Branwell. By 2 November Charlotte and Emily received a letter telling them that their aunt was dangerously ill. They immediately decided to return home to Haworth but the next day brought news of their aunt's agonising death. They dutifully returned home, their aunt having already been buried close to her sister before her nieces made it to Haworth.

Over Christmas 1842 the Brontë family took stock. Anne would stay as a governess with the Robinson family at Thorpe Green and Branwell would join her as a tutor to their son, Edmund. Branwell had been dismissed from his job as a railway clerk in circumstances which highlighted a careless attitude to his work. Emily, it seems, with relief, gladly accepted the role of family housekeeper and relished the freedom to write. All three nieces received under £300 each from their aunt's legacy.[6]

It was Charlotte who determined to hold on to her Continental dreams. She decided to take up M Heger's offer of a teaching post at the Pensionnat Heger and on 27 June 1843 she set off for London and the steam packet at London Bridge Wharf.

On arrival at Euston Station, she took a cab to London Bridge Wharf. If Charlotte's experience is mirrored in Lucy Snowe's experience in the novel *Villette* then Charlotte had a very frightening experience when she arrived at the Wharf. She writes that the cab man 'offered me up as an oblation, served me as a dripping roast, making me alight in the midst of a throng of watermen. This was an uncomfortable crisis. It was a dark night. The coachman instantly drove off as soon as he had got his fare; the watermen commenced a struggle for me and for my trunk. Their oaths I hear at this moment: they shook my philosophy more than did the night, or the isolation, or the strangeness of the scene.'[7]

Mrs Gaskell wrote of how Charlotte 'desired a waterman to row her to the Ostend packet, which was to sail the next morning.' She comments that Charlotte described to her, 'pretty much as she has since described it in *Villette* her sense of loneliness, and yet her strange pleasure in the excitement of the situation, as in the dead of that winter's night she went swiftly over the dark river to the black hull's side, and was at first refused leave to ascend to the deck. "No passengers might sleep on board," they said, with some appearance of disrespect. She looked back to the lights and subdued noises of London – that "Mighty Heart" in which she had no place, and, standing up in the rocking boat, she asked to speak to some one in authority on board the packet. He came, and her quiet simple statements of her wish, and her reason for it, quelled the feeling of sneering distrust in those who had first heard her request, and impressed the authority so favourably that he allowed her to come on board, and take possession of a berth.'[8] Charlotte set sail for the Continent the next morning, sailing right into one of the deepest and greatest emotional crisis of her entire life.

There are degrees of loneliness that human beings suffer but Charlotte Brontë was now to feel an isolation and loneliness that was to become a literary masterpiece. When she returned to the Heger Pensionnat she began to give English lessons. She was called Mademoiselle Charlotte by M Heger's orders. That she respected him and honoured him is certain. That he thought highly of her as one of his most talented pupils is also certain.

They got deeply into intellectual discussion through the essays she wrote on the subject of genius.[9]   Charlotte genuinely believed genius to be an innate gift from God. M Heger believed the same but that genius needs 'discipline and self control to achieve its potential.' Heger slowly won her around to his opinion that genius needed the study of past writers or artists to hone its talent. Just, he argued, as the gem-carver does not make the diamond, it is also important to recognise that without him the most beautiful diamond is a pebble.[10]

Heger knew very well the kind of unique talent he was dealing with in Charlotte and he helped and encouraged it. He drew her talent out and sought to channel it into even greater expression.   She was hugely vulnerable and, as the year progressed, her distinct lack of affection and dislike for the pupils and teachers in her school did not apply to M Heger. The truth is, as letters Charlotte wrote to M Heger after she had left Brussels (found at the beginning of the 20th century) prove, she had begun to fall in love with him. Perhaps it was, at first, unconscious, perhaps suppressed, but, as Juliet Barker points out, during the course of 1843 Charlotte 'slipped from normal feelings of respect and esteem for her teacher into an unhealthy and obsessive dependency on M Heger's every expression of approval.'[11]

As the situation progressed it now seems that M Heger's wife Zoë recognised Charlotte's attachment to her husband and that they both began to distinctly distance themselves from her. Charlotte suspected that Mme Heger was spying on her through the treachery of another teacher. To compound her loneliness, English families with whom Charlotte was friendly, namely the Dicksons and the Jenkins, left the city during the year and now, during the long five-week school summer holidays she was virtually alone at the Pensionnat Heger.

She was, Mrs Gaskell notes, 'left in the great deserted Pensionnat, with only one teacher for a companion. This teacher, a Frenchwoman, had always been uncongenial to her, but, left to each other's sole companionship, Charlotte soon discovered that her associate was more profligate, more steeped in a kind of cold, systematic sensuality than she had before imagined it possible for a human being to be, and her whole nature revolted from this woman's society. A low nervous fever was gaining upon Miss Brontë. She had never been a good sleeper but now she could not sleep at all.'[12]

When eventually Charlotte came to write her novel *Villette* it was to contain a study of what isolation does to a person psychologically. Victorian fiction contains no more emotionally harrowing writing.[13]

The following passage from *Villette* is clearly drawn from Charlotte's feelings during those summer holidays of 1843 in Brussels: 'My heart almost died within me, miserable longings strained its chords. How long were the September days! How silent, how lifeless! How vast and void seemed the desolate premises! How gloomy the forsaken garden - grey now with the dust of a town summer departed. Looking forward at the commencement of those eight weeks, I hardly knew how I was to live to the end. My spirits had long been gradually sinking; now that the prop of employment was withdrawn, they went down fast. Even to look forward was not to hope: the dumb future spoke no comfort, offered no promise, gave no inducement to bear present evil in reliance on future good.

'A sorrowful indifference to existence often pressed on me; a despairing resignation to reach betimes the end of all things earthly. Alas! when I had full leisure to look on life as life must be looked on by such as me, I found it but a hopeless desert: tawny sands, with no green fields, no palm trees, no well in view.

The hopes which are dear to youth, which bear it up and lead it on, I knew not and dared not know. If they knocked at my heart sometimes, an inhospitable bar to admission must be inwardly drawn. When they turned away thus rejected, tears sad enough sometimes flowed; but it could not be helped, I dared not give such guests lodging. So mortally did I fear the sin and weakness of presumption.

'Religious reader, you will preach to me a long sermon about what I have just written, and so will you, moralist; and you, stern sage; you, stoic, will frown; you, cynic, sneer; you, epicure, laugh. Well, each and all, take it your own way. I accept the sermon, frown, sneer, and laugh; perhaps you are all right, and perhaps, circumstanced like me, you would have been, like me, wrong. The first month was, indeed, a long, black, heavy month to me.'[14]

That summer Charlotte did something that proved to be completely out of character with her life before the incident and ever after. She later wrote to Emily describing what had happened. During that summer in her loneliness Charlotte had, Mrs Gaskell states, 'tried to walk herself into such a state of bodily fatigue as would induce sleep. So she went out, and with weary steps would traverse the boulevards and the streets, sometimes for hours together, faltering and resting occasionally on some of the many benches placed for the repose of happy groups, or for solitary wanderers like herself. Then up again, anywhere but to the Pensionnat, out to the cemetery where Martha lay, out beyond it, to the hills whence there is nothing to be seen but fields as far as the horizon. The shades of evening made her retrace her footsteps – sick for want of food, but not hungry; fatigued with long continued exercise – yet restless still, and doomed to another weary, haunted night of sleeplessness.'[15]

One evening, as she informed Emily, on her way back from the Protestant cemetery outside Brussels where Martha Taylor's grave was situated, Charlotte had what she called an 'odd whim'. On passing the great Cathedral of Ste Gudule at the time of the evening prayer service called Vespers, Charlotte entered the Cathedral and noted some people kneeling by the confessionals. She 'took a fancy' to change herself 'into a Catholic and go and make a real confession to see what it was like.'

When the priest opened the little wooden door inside the grating and lent his ear towards Charlotte, she told the priest that she was a foreigner and had been brought up a Protestant. When he asked her if she was a Protestant, she replied, 'yes'. He told her if that was so she could not join in the confession. Seeing that Charlotte was determined, though, to confess, the priest said he would allow it 'because it might be the first step towards returning to the true church.' Charlotte then made a real confession.

The priest gave Charlotte his address instructing her to come to his home every morning, promising he would reason with her and try to convince her of 'the error and enormity of being a Protestant.' Charlotte promised faithfully to go. 'Of course,' as Charlotte told Emily, 'the adventure stops there, and I hope I shall never see the priest again.'[17]

It was a rare juxtaposition for the author who would write *The Professor*. Patricia Ingham notes that in the novel the Belgian schoolgirl, Sylvie, represents 'what was to be feared by a female victim of Jesuitical priests.' She 'allowed control of her mind and body to pass into the hands of some despotic confessor.'[17]

'She permitted herself no original opinion, no preference of companion or employment; in everything she was guided by another ... she went about all day long doing what she was bid;

never what she liked, or what, from innate conviction she thought it right to do. The poor little future religieuse had been early taught to make the dictates of her own reason and conscience quite subordinate to the will of her spiritual director.'[18]

In *Villette* Charlotte makes her heroine Lucy Snowe go through her own experience at the Cathedral and writes: 'Did I, do you suppose, contemplate venturing again within that worthy priest's reach? As soon should I have thought of walking into a Babylonish furnace.' She continues: 'Had I gone to him, he would have shown me all that was tender, and comforting, and gentle, in the honest Popish superstition. Then he would have tried to kindle, blow and stir up in me the zeal of good works. I know not how it would all have ended. We all think ourselves strong in some points; we all know ourselves weak in many; the probabilities are that had I visited Numéro 10 Rue des Mages, at the hour and day appointed, I might just now, instead of writing this heretic narrative, be counting my beads in the cell of a certain Carmelite convent on the Boulevard of Crécy, in Villette. There was something of Fénélon about that benign old priest and, whatever most of his brethren may be, and whatever I may think of his Church and creed (and I like neither), of himself I must ever retain a grateful recollection. He was kind when I needed kindness; he did me good. May Heaven bless him!'[19]

Charlotte had a lifelong aversion to Catholicism. It has been suggested that this was fuelled by a fear that 'she might succumb to the very forms she logically rejected.'[20] The Fénélon she refers to in *Villette* is the famous seventeenth century Roman Catholic orator and later Archbishop who gave part of his time to trying to convert Huguenots to Catholicism and who was also noted for his great kindness which led many to convert to Catholicism.

Did Charlotte come close to conversion to the Catholic Church that lonely evening in Brussels? Her 'subsequent virulent antipathy to everything Catholic and particularly her abhorrence of the Catholic priesthood'[21] surely does not show a secret love of Catholicism but rather a fear that she could be seduced intellectually, emotionally, and spiritually into its fold against her conviction. It is, though, a kindly but now more cautious hand that wrote of Lucy Snowe's view of the priest at the Cathedral: 'He was kind when I needed kindness; he did me good. May Heaven bless him.'

The fascinating question is: 'What did Charlotte confess to?' Something was heavy on her mind to drive her to share it with someone else. In life, it is often the complete stranger, someone right outside of the disturbing circumstance who can lend a sympathetic ear and insightful mind to its complexities. In this case it was a priest who, though motivated by a desire to draw Charlotte into the Catholic faith, listened to her confession of some sin in her life. Did she confess to falling in love with M Heger? We will never know. She certainly didn't tell Emily when she wrote to her of the incident. She did, understandably, write: 'I think you had better not tell papa of this. He will not understand that it was only a freak, and will perhaps think I am going to turn Catholic.'[22]

The anguish that Charlotte now endured was deep. She desperately wanted to go home and, yet, in writing to Emily on the matter she dwelt poignantly on the fact that she had no 'fixed prospect' or 'pretext' to do so.[23] She tried to bring things to a head by giving her notice to Zoë Heger but when M Heger heard about it he forbade her to leave. He offered to teach her arithmetic to which she had pleaded much ignorance. The course began but even this did not work out.

Charlotte's abhorrence of Zoë Heger was reaching boiling point and she famously described her to Ellen Nussey as being one who 'seems a rosy sugar plum but I know her to be coloured chalk.'[24] She is, of course, the model for Mme Beck in *Villette* who is Jesuitical. Looked at fairly and impartially, though, Mme Heger must have known that Charlotte's infatuation with her husband could have led to a serious scandal leading to the ruination not only of her family but the Pensionnat and both her own and her husband's careers.

Charlotte's spirits got lower and lower and, mercifully, she finally decided to leave Brussels and return home. With a breaking heart Charlotte said her goodbyes to Constantin Heger. He gave her a diploma, sealed with the seal of the Athénée Royal that gave testimony to her teaching abilities. On Sunday 31 December, the last day of 1843, Charlotte Brontë left the city where the greatest adventure in her life was to give birth, in one's opinion, to her most mature writing. As Zoë Heger accompanied Charlotte to the boat at Ostend, Charlotte was on her way to prove with her pen that the sweetest songs are those of saddest thought.

What kind of parsonage did Charlotte return to? Her father continued to remain very active, though now sixty-six-years-of-age. He had been campaigning against nationalist movements in Ireland, Scotland and Wales.[25] In a letter to his brother Hugh in Ireland, he argued that Protestants should arm and organise themselves within the law against rebellion and warned of dire consequences if Catholics got to power.[26] He denounced duelling in the *Leeds Mercury* stating that it was wrong on biblical as well as practical grounds.[27] He called for an Act of Parliament that would make it an offence to give or accept a challenge; he even went as far as stating that he felt the punishment for the offence should be transportation for life.[28]

Such campaigning against duelling shows that Patrick Brontë was right at the heart of the reforming evangelical movement of the eighteenth and nineteenth century. He was following in the footsteps of his former sponsor, William Wilberforce, who took deep objection to his close friend, the Prime Minister William Pitt, fighting a duel on Putney Heath on Whitsunday 1798 with an Irish Member of Parliament called George Tierney. Wilberforce believed that Pitt had put his private feelings before duty to his country and to God. He put down a motion in Parliament to outlaw duelling and only withdrew it when Pitt told him it would force his resignation because he had been a duellist; Wilberforce believed that Pitt was the best national leader at the time.[29]

Patrick had also worked hard at improving education in Haworth and, as Charlotte returned, a new National School was opened on 2 June 1844 under the auspices of Patrick's church.[30] He was also campaigning in a newspaper against the dangers of fire. He stated that he had buried as many as between ninety and one hundred children in Haworth who had been burnt to death when their clothes caught fire. He spoke against the parental neglect which led to the deaths of children by fire and urged that children should be encouraged to wear silk and woollen clothing rather than cotton and linen which were hugely flammable.[31]

Charlotte found Emily running the Brontë parsonage efficiently with the help of Tabby Akroyd who, though hindered by age and lameness, had returned to help where she could. Emily continued to write poetry and the world and power of imagination remained undimmed in her life. She was showing signs of being tempted by Pantheism. Anne continued to teach at Thorpe Green and Branwell had also continued there as a tutor. Anne's poetry continued to flourish though loneliness.

At times, spiritual uncertainty and doubt rose up to plague her. She longed and pleaded for a strong, doubt-free faith and took a strong stance for belief in the decidedly unbiblical and unevangelical idea of universal salvation. Her father would have strongly disagreed. In his funeral sermon for the Rev William Weightman, for example, he had made it clear that Christ's atonement had opened the door of salvation to everybody. He also pointed out that 'the mere existence of an open door was not enough – redemption does not extend to him or her who shows no interest in going through it.'[32] According to Paul's letter to the *Romans* the righteousness of God that is available through faith is, after all, 'unto all and upon all them that *believe:* for there is no difference for all have sinned and come short of the glory of God; being justified freely by his grace through the redemption that is in Christ Jesus.'[33]

Anne's devotion to her daily teaching responsibilities continued to be absolute despite her loneliness and fear. What then of the school the Brontë sisters had spoken of founding? In the summer of 1844 Charlotte decided that she would open her school in the parsonage with around half a dozen pupils. She wrote around to her contacts looking for possible pupils; in the end, although people thought the school a good idea, the remoteness of Haworth was a distinct disadvantage. Charlotte had cards printed which advertised, 'The Misses Brontë's Establishment' and had them circulated with Ellen Nussey's help; ultimately, though, the project was abandoned. The pupils loss would be literature's gain.

Charlotte had arrived home to find that her father's eyesight was failing rapidly and that his curate, the Rev James Smith, was not proving to be a success. She herself was deeply depressed and even hypochondriac. She continued writing fervid letters to Constantin Heger but he wisely stopped writing to her, keeping his distance. Charlotte continued writing to him until 1845 but, though she waited day by day for an answer, it never came.

In November 1845 the pain of her feelings come across in a letter where she cries: 'To forbid me to write to you, to refuse to answer me, would be to tear me from my only joy on earth ... When day by day I await a letter, and when day by day disappointment comes ... l lose appetite and sleep – I pine away.'[34]

There is a tradition in the Heger family that Constantin Heger eventually tore some of Charlotte's letters and put them in a wastepaper basket. It seems that Zoë Heger retrieved them and stitched them together again. They were eventually given by Heger's son, Dr Paul Heger, to the British Museum where they are now available for public study.[35]

A poem telling of a self-centred man who rejects his devoted lover was written by Charlotte in January 1845, and states:

His coming was my hope each day
His parting was my pain!
The chance that did his steps delay
Was ice in every vein.

The obsession with Heger is perhaps capsulated by the final verse of the poem:

The truest love that ever heart,
Felt at its kindled core;
Through every vein with quickened start,
A tide of life did pour.[36]

Charlotte's depression with what she perceived to be her narrow circumstances was compounded when her close friend Mary Taylor emigrated to New Zealand in March 1845. Feeling hemmed in, she considered going to Paris as a governess.[37] When Anne returned for the summer holidays and conveyed to her family that she had resigned her post with the Robinsons, this freed Charlotte to accept an invitation from Ellen Nussey to go for a holiday to Hathersage in Derbyshire. Ellen's brother Henry, now the vicar of Hathersage, had married and Ellen was staying at the vicarage to prepare it for the couple who were on honeymoon. Charlotte took wings and stayed in Hathersage for three weeks with huge literary consequences.

Hathersage was to become the fictional village of Morton in *Jane Eyre*; the Peak scenery around it was to become the landscape for the River's cottage in the novel; the four medieval brasses in St Michael's Church in Hathersage dedicated to the Eyre family seems to have given Charlotte the surname for her heroine. The Eyre home at nearby North Lees Hall, may have inspired Mr Rochester's Thornfield Hall. Even the landscape across which Charlotte travelled on the moorlands between Sheffield and Hathersage became the landscape for Jane Eyre's flight from Rochester. It was all probably subconscious with Charlotte at the time. The fact that she was living in a house belonging to the man who had so coldly proposed to her and who had thought of becoming a missionary was probably firing Charlotte's subconscious, later to surface in the character of the Rev St John Rivers in *Jane Eyre*.

Whatever was going on in Charlotte's subconscious at the time certainly did not prepare her for the full-blown crisis she returned to at Haworth parsonage. She got home at 10.00 on a Saturday night to find, as she put it to her friend Ellen, that Branwell was 'ill.' This was probably a euphemism for 'drunk.' Commenting on his 'illness', she wrote: 'He is so, very often, owing to his own fault.'[38] Charlotte further explained to Ellen the reason for his present state. He had, Anne had told her, on the previous Thursday received a note from Mr Robinson sternly dismissing him from his post as tutor to his son Edmund Robinson Junior. His behaviour had been 'bad beyond expression' and he had been charged to break off all communication with any member of the Robinson family.[39]

A lot of speculative writing has emerged from Brontë scholars regarding Branwell's behaviour which was to have huge implications on the Brontë family. All in all, most accept that Branwell had an affair with Mrs Robinson. Charlotte's biographer, Mrs Gaskell, certainly believed he did, as did his family. Branwell screamed his love for Mrs Robinson in drunken stupors all over Haworth.[40]

Did Anne resign her post because of her brother's behaviour in the Robinson household? Evidence points to the fact that it was probably disgust with Mrs Robinson and her children that prompted her resignation rather than the fear that her brother's behaviour would be exposed.

Patrick was no biblical Eli with his immoral son. He opposed what he did and remonstrated with him not to carry on any further communication with Mrs Robinson. Branwell defied his father's remonstrance.

Branwell continued to write poetry even after the debacle with the Robinson family, having two poems published in the *Halifax Guardian* in the winter of 1845.[41] He even set about writing a novel for publication, being the first Brontë to do so.[42] It was never finished and, in fact, his affair with Mrs Robinson spelled his ruin. His life was now truly set on a downward spiralling course that was to bring distress, not to speak of constant dreary disruption to life at the parsonage. Charlotte was contemptuous of Branwell's behaviour; Emily, at most, pitied him; and, out of it all, Anne was to write *The Tenant of Wildfell Hall.*

So often, though, great things turn on tiny incidents and in the eye of the storm at Haworth parsonage, Charlotte found a notebook in the autumn of 1845. As a result, the life of the Brontës and their legacy was to begin to tentatively move out into the ages.

NINE

Did You Want to See Me, Ma'am?

ONE DAY in the autumn of 1845 Charlotte Brontë accidentally lighted upon a notebook of her sister Emily's poems. Immediately, she was seized with a deep conviction that these were 'not common effusions, not at all like the poetry women generally write.' She thought them 'condensed and terse, vigorous and genuine.' To her ear, 'they also had a peculiar music – wild, melancholy, and elevating.'

Aware that her sister 'was not a person of demonstrative character, nor one, on the recesses of whose mind and feelings, even those nearest and dearest to her could, with impunity intrude unlicensed,' Charlotte, nevertheless, made an attempt. She freely admitted that it took hours to reconcile Emily to the discovery she had made and days to persuade her that 'such poems merited publication.'

As Charlotte sought to fan Emily's poetic spark to a flame, Anne quickly produced some of her own compositions intimating that since Emily's poems had given her pleasure, she might like to look at hers!

Initially raging at the intrusion, Emily, eventually, gave in. Under pressure from Emily and Anne, Charlotte agreed that the poems should be published under pseudonyms. 'Averse to personal publicity,' wrote Charlotte, 'we veiled our names under those of Currer, Ellis and Acton Bell; the ambiguous choice being dictated by a sort of conscientious scruple at assuming Christian names positively masculine, while we did not like to declare ourselves women, because – without at that time suspecting that our mode of writing and thinking was not what is called "feminine" – we had a vague impression that authoresses are liable to be looked on with prejudice; we had noticed how critics sometimes use for their chastisement the weapon of personality, and for them reward, a flattery which is not true praise.'[1] In their choice of pseudonyms, each sister retained their own initials.

That autumn they set to work choosing their poems. Charlotte contributed nineteen, Anne and Emily twenty-one each. On 28 June 1846 they were submitted to the small publishing house of Alyott and Jones at No. 8 Paternoster Row, London. Eventually, after a good deal of correspondence from Charlotte as to print, format, paper and review copies, *Poems* by Currer, Ellis and Acton Bell surfaced from Alyott and Jones in May 1846, paid for by ten guineas from each sister, later increased by one sum of £5.[2]

As Mrs Gaskell put it, the book of poems, 'stole into life: some weeks passed over, without the mighty murmuring public discovering that three more voices were uttering their speech.' In the *Athenaeum* the reviewer assigned Ellis, 'the highest rank of the three "brothers."'[3]   Two other reviewers praised the work and the general public ignored it.[4] One year after its publication, let all inspiring writers note, it had sold all of two copies!

The Brontë sisters, completely undeterred, now turned to write fiction.   Over that winter and spring Emily wrote *Wuthering Heights*, Anne wrote *Agnes Grey*, and Charlotte wrote *The Professor*. One thing is certain, a hungry public did not inspire them! They hoped that the three novels would be published together and each was written, Mrs Gaskell tells us, in collaboration. Each girl read passages aloud to each other and discussed their characters and plots as they paced up and down the sitting room.[5]

That their imagination soared despite all that surrounded them beggars description. Yet, is it not so in the history of literature that narrow circumstances often trigger great writing? As Sinead Smyth has accurately observed, 'oppressed people fantasise.' A further distressing circumstance now grew in the form of a cataract impairing Patrick Brontë's eyesight. He was now nearly blind. He continued to preach but could no longer see to read. 'I have heard,' wrote Mrs Gaskell, 'that he was led up into the pulpit, and that his sermons were never so effective as when he stood there, a grey sightless old man, his blind eyes looking out straight before him, while the words that came from his lips had all the vigour and force of his best days.'[6]

In July, Emily and Charlotte went to Manchester to see a famous oculist called William James Wilson. He could not tell from their description whether Patrick's eyes were ready for an operation or not. So it was that Charlotte took her father to Manchester in August 1846 and, after a favourable prognosis, they settled at No. 83 Mount Pleasant, Boundary Street, off the Oxford Road in Manchester for the next month. These lodgings, recommended by Mr Wilson, were kept by an old servant of his who was ill and who had gone out into the country.

The operation took place on 26 August and Charlotte wrote to Ellen: 'Mr Wilson says, he considers it quite successful; but papa cannot yet see anything. The affair lasted precisely a quarter of an hour ... papa displayed extraordinary patience and firmness; the surgeons seemed surprised.'[7] The operation was, of course, conducted without anaesthetic. Charlotte, at her father's wish, was present in the room during the operation.

Following the operation Patrick was confined to his bed in a dark room with the instructions that he was to speak and to be spoken to as little as possible. He was not to be stirred for four days. A nurse was on hand and Charlotte, with time on her hands, and enduring sleepless nights with a raging toothache[8] took up her pencil and wrote: 'There was no possibility of taking a walk that day.'[9] *Jane Eyre* was born! While his daughter saw far horizons in her moral tale of the plain, small and physically unattractive governess who fell in love with a married man, Patrick had his bandages removed and began the journey of recovering his sight.

After working on *Jane Eyre* with unremitting fervency for five weeks in Manchester, Charlotte and her father returned to Howarth at the end of September 1846. By November, to Patrick's unbounded relief and joy, his sight had so recovered that he was able to return to his pulpit and parish duties once more.

While Patrick had joy in his pulpit, Charlotte had joy at the parsonage, continuing to write her novel. For three weeks she was caught up in an incredible flow of creative writing in little square paper books, held close to her eyes because of her short-sightedness, and written in the first copy in pencil.[10] Here surfaces the character of the shy but passionate Jane and the intelligent, spiritual and turning-the-other-cheek Helen Burns.

The romantic, arrogant and dangerous Rochester is set against his hidden but ever-present cunning and insane wife, Bertha. The austere, inflexible, cold Rev St John Rivers and the tyrannical, power-mad, punishment-obsessed Rev Brocklehurst represent a none-too-pleasant view of clergymen. The vain, malicious, beautiful, self-possessed, arrogant Blanche Ingram is everything that the plain, down-to-earth Jane is not. In the 21st century the writer A N Wilson has said: '*Jane Eyre* is not merely a justly popular novel. It is one of the great documents of 19th century Protestantism.'[11] It is even more than that. It is a novel which explores in detail the very nature of Christianity itself, particularly Christian morality.

What must have been going on in Charlotte's mind and heart as she describes her heroine Jane refusing to go and live with Rochester after she discovers the existence of his wife Bertha? That discovery was made, of course, at the church altar within seconds of Jane being married to Rochester. It is the most famous church wedding service in fiction. Here, though, was Charlotte writing the story of Jane's refusal to live with the married Rochester while at the same time Charlotte was in love with a married man herself, albeit, he was not pleading with her to live with him. Jane's turning away from immorality was surely Charlotte's own personal and brilliant exposition of how she felt about the law of God regarding love and marriage. Charlotte knew very well that the Bible taught that righteousness exalts a nation but that sin is a reproach to any people.[12] In Jane's refusal of Rochester we can feel the pulse of Charlotte Brontë for not only is *Jane Eyre* one of fiction's greatest love stories, it is also deeply autobiographical, particularly at this point.

Jane weighs up in her mind her situation, admitting to herself how easy it would be to comply with Rochester's pleadings: '... while he spoke my very conscience and reason turned traitors against me, and charged me with crime in resisting him. They spoke almost as loud as Feeling, and that clamoured wildly, "Oh, comply!" it said. "Think of his misery; think of his danger; look at his state when left alone; remember his headlong nature; consider his recklessness following on despair – soothe him; save him; love him; tell him you love him and will be his. Who in the world cares for *you*? or who will be injured by what you do?"

'Still indomitable was the reply, "*I* care for myself. The more solitary, the more friendless, the more unsustained I am, the more I will respect myself. I will keep the law given by God; sanctioned by man. I will hold to the principles received by me when I was sane and not mad, as I am now. Laws and principles are not for the times when there is no temptation: they are for such moments as this, when body and soul rise in mutiny against their rigour; stringent are they; inviolate they shall be. If at my individual convenience I might break them, what would be their worth? They have a worth, so I have always believed; and if I cannot believe it now, it is because I am insane – quite insane, with my veins running fire, and my heart beating faster than I can count its throbs. Preconceived opinions, foregone determinations, are all I have at this hour to stand by: there I plant my foot." I did. Mr Rochester reading my countenance, saw I had done so.'[13]

Charlotte balances her novel with Jane also turning away from St John Rivers when he wants to make her his missionary wife and to serve with her in India. One wonders if Charlotte is not dealing with institutionalised rape disguised with doing the will of God? The Rev St John Rivers is not in the least in love with Jane and, as she puts it, 'has no more of a husband's heart for me than that frowning giant of a rock, down which the stream is foaming in yonder gorge. He prizes me as a soldier would a good weapon, and that is all.'[14]

She refuses him with as much vigour as she did Rochester. His behaviour is held up to scorn in *Jane Eyre* every bit as much as the profligate Rochester's behaviour if, albeit, his sincerity in seeking to serve God in missionary service in India is admired: '... but can I let him complete his calculations, coolly put into practice his plans, go through the wedding ceremony? Can I receive from him the bridal ring, endure all forms of love (which I doubt not he would scrupulously observe) and know that the spirit was quite absent? Can I bear the consciousness that every endearment he bestows is a sacrifice made on principle? No, such a martyrdom would be monstrous. I will never undergo it. As his sister, I might accompany him, not as his wife; I will tell him so.'[15]

There is no more revealing paragraph in Charlotte's writing than what Jane thinks of St John River's preaching: 'Throughout there was strange bitterness; an absence of consolatory gentleness; stern allusions to Calvinistic doctrines – election, predestination, reprobation – were frequent; and each reference to these points sounded like a sentence pronounced for doom. When he had done, instead of feeling better, calmer, more enlightened by his discourse, I experienced an inexpressible sadness; for it seemed to me – I know not whether equally so to others – that the eloquence to which I had been listening had sprang from a depth where lay turbid dregs of disappointment, where moved troubling impulses of insatiate yearnings and disquieting aspirations. I was sure St John Rivers, pure-lived, conscientious, zealous as he was, had not yet found the peace of God which passeth all understanding ...'[16]

One of English literature's most memorable lines starts *Jane Eyre's* last chapter: 'Reader, I married him.'[17] The blinded Rochester repents and is found standing worshipping God, saying: 'I thank my Maker, that, in the midst of judgment, he has remembered mercy. I humbly entreat my Redeemer to give me strength to lead henceforth a purer life than I have done hitherto!'[18] It is the balance of Charlotte's writing about love, sex, passion and morality that gives her novel its universal appeal even in the 21st century.

After a three-week surge of intense creativity, Charlotte paused, took a creative breath and returned to her creation at a slower, less vehement pace 'with more anxious care', as her friend Harriet Martineau noted.[19] Many readers have felt the first part of her novel is actually better than the second.

While Charlotte worked on her masterpiece, Branwell's life continued to deteriorate. His lover's husband had died but she showed no interest in marrying him. He continued to write poetry, drew wild sketches and spent time in Halifax, it seems, with his friend J B Leyland.[20] He was visited by the Sheriff's Officer and told to pay his drinking debts or he would be sent to the Debtors Prison at York.[21]

Given some money secretly by his former lover, Branwell continued to slip further into dependence on alcohol and opiates as the severe winter of 1846 closed in.[22] It brought colds and coughs at the parsonage and severe distressing asthma to the uncomplaining Anne.[23]

The pivotal year of 1847, literary-wise, saw Patrick campaigning in the papers for compulsory national education,[24] and, understandably, the use of ether for surgical operations, which, he said, 'ought to be patronised by every friend to humanity.'[25] With insight and visionary fervour he also campaigned for the appointment of godly young subdeacons to church work, who could be drawn, he suggested, from the ranks of well-educated parish clerks and schoolmasters.[26]   He even wrote an amazing poem about the Rev Nicholls' victory over the washerwomen of Howarth in preventing them spreading out their wet sheets and laundry on the tombstones in Howarth churchyard to dry![27]   It was obvious that Patrick was relishing his ability to read and write once more.

Sadly, Branwell's last re-drafted poem was published in the *Halifax Guardian* on 5 June 1847 mirroring his own relentless slide to death. It was titled, *The End of All ...*

In that unpitying winter's night
When my own wife – my Mary – died,
I, by my fire's declining light,
Sat comfortless, and silent sighed.
While burst, unchecked, grief's bitter tide,
As I, methought, when she was gone,
Not hours, but years like this must bide,
And wake, and weep, and watch alone ...

I could not bear the thoughts which rose,
Of what had been and what must be,
But still the dark night would disclose
Its sorrow-pictured prophecy:
Still saw I – miserable me,
Long – long nights else – in lonely gloom,
With time-bleached locks and trembling knee,
Walk aidless – hopeless – to my tomb.[28]

The highs and lows of the Brontë family continued throughout the year. For Emily and Anne a pivotal high came when *Wuthering Heights* and *Agnes Grey* were accepted for publication in one volume by a minor publisher, T C Newby. The acceptance came with the proviso that the authors advanced £50.[29] The thought that a multi-million dollar film entitled *Brontë*, directed and written by Charles Sturridge would be made of the lives of the Brontë sisters at the beginning of the 21st century, never to speak of the films that have been made of their novels or the books written about them, would never have crossed their minds. Such is the world of creativity; little acorns become mighty oaks.

In July 1847, Charlotte wrote to the publishing house of Smith, Elder & Co. having had her novel *The Professor* turned down by six other publishers.[30] It must have taken unrelenting optimism to post that package, but her seventh attempt to have her novel published brought an unexpected response. While they declined to publish *The Professor*, they stated that they would give careful attention to a work of three volumes that she might present. They also carefully discussed the merits and demerits of *The Professor* in a way that gave the oxygen of encouragement to Charlotte at a time when she was in dire need of it.[31]

Smith, Elder & Co., of course, were unaware that *Jane Eyre* was being written and, duly on 24 August, the fair copy of the final manuscript was sent by rail from Keighley.[32] As the train carried Charlotte's precious manuscript towards Smith, Elder & Co. and eventual worldwide fame in the annals of English literature, what was it at its heart that has proved so captivating?

Mrs Gaskell wisely chose the words of a writer who penned a beautiful obituary when Charlotte eventually died to capture the essence of the novel's allure: 'She once told her sisters that they were wrong – even morally wrong – in making their heroines beautiful as a matter of course. They replied that it was impossible to make a heroine interesting on any other terms. Her answer was: "I will prove to you that you are wrong; I will show you a heroine as plain and as small as myself, who shall be as interesting as any of yours!" Hence *Jane Eyre,* said she, in telling the anecdote, "but she is not myself, any further than that."[33]

The modern age's obsession with the cult of celebrity based on 'the beautiful people' could do with a good dose of Charlotte's doctrine. One could define it as contending that you can be beautiful without being good looking.

When George Smith of Smith, Elder & Co. eventually got to read Charlotte's novel he told how he had made an appointment to meet a friend on the Sunday morning, hoping to ride to meet him at some two to three miles distance. At twelve noon his groom arrived at his house with his horse for the journey. Smith was so engrossed in the novel that he dismissed his groom, sending him off with a note for his friend telling him that circumstances had arisen to prevent his meeting him! When called to lunch, he asked for a sandwich and a drink to be sent to him and he read on. Even eventual dinner became a hurried one and before he slept he had the manuscript finished.[34]

Smith, Elder & Co. offered Charlotte £100 for the copyright to her book on the condition that they had right of refusal to her next two books for which she was offered £100 each.[35] They also suggested that Charlotte rewrite the section on Lowood School. To her everlasting credit she refused, arguing that what she had written was the truth even though she had held back some of the more painful particulars.[36] How dark her Lowood days must have been!

Jane Eyre was published in October 1847 and it must have been with a thumping heart that Charlotte, urged on by her sisters, decided one afternoon to tell her father of its publication. The latter told Mrs Gaskell of his reaction and she wrote it down as follows:

'Papa, I've been writing a book.'

'Have you, my dear?'

'Yes, and I want you to read it.'

'I am afraid it will try my eyes too much.'

'But it is not in manuscript, it is printed.'

'My dear! You've never thought of the expense it will be! It will be almost sure to be a loss, for how can you get a book sold? No one knows you or your name.'

'But, papa, I don't think it will be a loss; no more will you, if you'll just let me read you a review or two, and tell you more about it.'

Charlotte told how she sat down and read some of the reviews to her father; and then, giving him the copy of *Jane Eyre* that she intended for him, she left him to read it. When he came in to tea, he said: 'Girls, do you know Charlotte has been writing a book, and it is much better than likely?'[37]

Much better than likely? William Makepeace Thackeray said it was the first English novel he'd been able to read for many a day. He said some of the love passages had made him cry.[38] He wasn't to be the last reader to be deeply moved by Charlotte's masterpiece. Millions have followed him.

Charlotte, of course, knew nothing of the fact that Thackeray had an insane wife and could clearly identify with Rochester's feelings. Fact was stranger than fiction. Charlotte dedicated the second edition of *Jane Eyre* to Thackeray and in the preface she defended her work which had sold out in three months. Her defence against the critics who had called her novel 'improper', 'godless' and 'pernicious' shows veins truly running fire. 'Conventionality is not morality. Self-righteousness is not religion. To attack the first is not to assail the last. To pluck the mask from the face of the Pharisee, is not to lift an impious hand to the Crown of Thorns. These things and deeds are diametrically opposed, they are as distinct as is vice from virtue. Men too often confound them, they should not be confounded; appearance should not be mistaken for truth; narrow human doctrines, that only tend to elate and magnify a few, should not be substituted for the world-redeeming creed of Christ. There is – I repeat it – a difference; and it is a good, and not a bad action to mark broadly and clearly the line of separation between them.'[39]

Poor Charlotte now came under the embarrassment of widespread gossip in London that Currer Bell had been a governess in Thackeray's home! In December 1847, Emily's *Wuthering Heights* and Anne's *Agnes Grey* were finally published by T C Newby of Cavendish Square, London. We are told that *Wuthering Heights* positively frightened Charlotte and, no wonder; the ferocity of feelings described in the book would frighten anyone.

It is a tale of the Earnshaw's, farmers for three hundred years, being at The Heights on the edge of the moors. In the more genteel and cosier Thorncross Grange down the valley lived the less fierce Lintons. Mr Earnshaw goes to Liverpool and brings back a dark-skinned homeless gypsy whom they name Heathcliff and, as Phyllis Bentley put it, 'jealousy, hatred, a passion almost too fierce to be called love ensued; the persecuted Heathcliff vanishes, returns rich, finds his Cathy married to a Linton, determines to ruin both families, and is only thwarted in the next generation by an honest decent love.'[40]

Here is another masterpiece of English literature that was to become, arguably, the most passionately original novel in the English language. It was Emily's only published novel and few other novels in English literature have ever been met with so much controversy, interest and critical analysis. That interest and analysis continues unabated. Emily did not give any relief in the haunting tale covering themes such as hate, revenge, gambling, excessive drinking, brutality, savagery, coarseness, disagreeable language and spirituality with raw, awesome imaginative power.

Some critics roundly condemned it, others saw the gifted writer behind the tale. It has been suggested that the character of Heathcliff is based on the story of Emily's great-grandfather, a cattle dealer in the River Boyne area. He often crossed the sea to Liverpool to trade and on one of his return trips a dark, dirty, half-naked boy was found in the hold of his ship. When no one could be found to give him medical attention or to care for him, Emily's great-great grandparents adopted him. The ensuing tale passed on to her family by Patrick had all the elements of cruelty, craftiness, scandal and revenge within it.[41] Whatever view is taken of Emily's largely amoral novel, one thing is agreed by most readers, here are some of the finest depictions of English landscape ever penned:

'Wuthering Heights is the name of Mr Heathcliff's dwelling; "Wuthering" being a significant provincial adjective, descriptive of the atmospheric tumult to which its station is exposed in stormy weather. Pure, bracing ventilation they must have up there, at all times, indeed: one may guess the power of the north wind, blowing over the edge, by the excessive slant of a few, stunted firs at the end of the house; and by a range of gaunt thorns all stretching their limbs one way, as if craving alms of the sun.'[42]

Even the very moors slip onto Catherine Earnshaw's grave. Who could forget Emily's description through the words of Nelly Dean?: 'The place of Catherine's interment, to the surprise of the villagers, was neither in the chapel, under the carved monument of the Lintons, nor yet by the tombs of her own relations, outside. It was dug on a green slope, in a corner of the kirkyard, where the wall is so low that heath and bilberry plants have climbed over it from the moor, and peat mould almost buries it. Her husband lies in the same spot, now; and they have each a simple headstone above, and a plain grey block at their feet, to mark the graves.'[43]

When Mr Lockwood decides to visit Thorncross Grange once more the landscape is described perfectly. Lockwood leaves his servant behind 'and proceeded down the valley alone. The grey church looked greyer, and the lonely churchyard lonelier. I distinguished a moor sheep cropping the short turf on the graves. It was sweet, warm weather – too warm for travelling; but the heat did not hinder me from enjoying the delightful scenery above and below; had I seen it nearer August, I'm sure it would have tempted me to waste a month among its solitudes. In winter, nothing more dreary; in summer, nothing more divine, than those glens shut in by hills, and those bluff, bold swells of heath.'[44]

When Mr Lockwood leaves Thorncross Grange to visit Wuthering Heights for the last time, Emily's description of his journey shows how deeply her consciousness has imbibed the natural world around her; every noun and adjective, every verb and adverb, every main or subordinated clause is drawn upon to create the atmosphere and the ambience of Mr Lockwood's journey.

Not finding Nelly Dean at Thorncross Grange, Mr Lockwood takes his journey: 'I would have asked why Mrs Dean had deserted the Grange, but it was impossible to delay her at such a crisis, so, I turned away and made my exit, rambling leisurely along with the glow of a sinking sun behind, and the mild glory of a rising moon in front; one fading, and the other brightening, as I quitted the park, and climbed the stony byroad branching off to Mr Heathcliff's dwelling. Before I arrived in sight of it, all that remained of day was a beamless, amber light along the west; but I could see every pebble on the path, and every blade of grass, by that splendid moon.'[45]

Was it a description of her own veins when Emily made Catherine cry to Heathcliff in the novel?: "'Oh, for mercy's sake," interrupted the mistress, stamping her foot, "for mercy's sake, let us hear no more of it now! Your cold blood cannot be worked into a fever – your veins are full of ice-water – but mine are boiling, and the sight of such chilliness makes them dance."'[46]

Reaction to Anne's novel, *Agnes Grey*, by reviewers was practically nil; the few who did react did not rate it very highly. The book's powerful exposé of the treatment of governesses by families of nobility, aristocracy and the upper classes though drew fire from her targets.

Anne was later to refer to the criticism in a preface she wrote in the second edition of her next novel, which she had begun probably in April 1847, *The Tenant of Wildfell Hall*: 'The story of *Agnes Grey* was accused of extravagant over-colouring in those very parts that were carefully copied from the life, with a most scrupulous avoidance of all exaggeration ...'[47]

Anne's depth of character and love of nature are apparent in the novel and, while the critics may not have encouraged her, she most certainly was not deterred to lift her pen again and write not for fame or fortune but with a definite moral purpose. Her next novel was to prove her very real versatility to write in a different style and format with more power.

Lucasta Miller has pointed out that *The Tenant of Wildfell Hall*, 'offended the shockable sections of society more than the other Brontë novels.' She writes that 'in its uncompromising attack on masculine vice and on the laws which bound a wife to an abusive husband, it offered a more explicit piece of social and moral criticism than can be found in the works of Charlotte or Emily.' She also points out that Anne, in her preface for the second edition, included the most explicit demand for equality for female writers to come from the Brontës: 'I am satisfied that if a book is a good one, it is so whatever the sex of the author may be ... I am at a loss to conceive how a man should permit himself to write anything that would be really disgraceful to a woman, or why a woman should be censured for writing anything that would be proper and becoming for a man.'[48]

In popular culture Anne is often stereotyped as gentle, delicate, slight, feminine, pretty and little. She has even been novelised as 'The Captive Dove'.[49] What rubbish! In her graphic portrayal of Arthur Huntingdon's bad language, drunkenness, violence and adultery and his attempts to corrupt his infant son, it is reckoned she is drawing from a thoroughly disreputable former Keighley curate, the Rev John Collins. Patrick had advised Collin's long suffering wife in 1840 to leave him and go to her home if she had one.[50] Six-and-a-half years later Mrs Collins turned up at the Haworth parsonage, pale and worn.

Taking tea with the Brontës she poured out the story of her appalling distresses. Collins had treated her and her child savagely and was a drunken, profligate hypocrite. He had followed an infamous career of vice in England and France including, it seems, giving his wife venereal disease and abandoning her with two children without any money in a lodging house in Manchester. Mrs Collins had bravely and successfully survived and overcome all her sorrows with hugely commendable dignity.[51]

It appears that Mrs Collin's story inspired Anne's novel *The Tenant of Wildfell Hall* for it is the story of Martha Huntington's brave survival of her horrendous marriage to a place of independence and great moral strength. It seems more than true that the drunkenness of Arthur Huntington was modeled on Branwell and it is clear from Charlotte's biographical notice that Anne had '... in the course of her life, been called to contemplate, near at hand and for a long time, the terrible effects of talents misused and faculties abused; hers was naturally a sensitive, reserved, and dejected nature; what she saw sank very deeply into her mind; it did her harm. She brooded over it till she believed it to be a duty to reproduce every detail (of course, with fictitious characters, incidents, and situations) as a warning to others. She hated her work, but would pursue it. When reasoned with on the subject, she regarded such reasonings as a temptation to self-indulgence. She must be honest; she must not varnish, soften, or conceal.'[52]

Charlotte's reaction in defending her sister when she faced fierce critical outrage on the publication of the book was to argue that 'her choice of subject was an entire mistake. Nothing less congruous with the writer's nature could be conceived.'[53]

All this has had the effect of hugely sidelining Anne from the posthumous Brontë reputation. Lucasta Miller has made the point that it is doubtful whether Charlotte 'truly and uncomplicatedly believed what she had said.'[54] Anne's novel now shines like a beacon in the 21st century as an encouragement to women in an abusive marriage, declaring that there is a future for them. They most certainly need a beacon for millions face every bit as much abuse as that depicted in *The Tenant of Wildfell Hall* and need to be assured that they do not need to continue to be a doormat upon which scoundrels can wipe their feet.

As for her depiction of the reality of what it is like to be in such a situation, she made no excuse. There is burning fire in Anne's veins as she writes in her preface to the second edition: '... those scenes which, I will venture to say, have not been more painful for the most fastidious of my critics to read, than they were for me to describe. I may have gone too far; in which case I shall be careful not to trouble myself or my readers in the same way again; but when we have to do with vice and vicious characters, I maintain it is better to depict them as they really are than as they would wish to appear.

'To represent a bad thing in its least offensive light is, doubtless, the most agreeable course for a writer of fiction to pursue; but is it the most honest, or the safest? Is it better to reveal the snares and pitfalls of life to the young and thoughtless traveller, or to cover them with branches and flowers? Oh, reader! if there were less of this delicate concealment of facts – this whispering, "Peace, peace," when there is no peace, there would be less of sin and misery to the young of both sexes who are left to wring their bitter knowledge from experience.'[55]

The beginning of the year 1848 saw Branwell continue to plunge further into the downward spiral of his life in Halifax inns.[56] He even set his bedclothes on fire while lying drunk in his bed. Anne discovered him and, when she couldn't raise him, she fled for Emily who dragged him out of bed and doused the flames.[57] This incident led to Patrick insisting that Branwell slept in his father's room.[58] It must have been a hell on earth for the old rector as Branwell was now experiencing tremors from his alcoholism.

Charlotte now turned, after serious thought, to write her novel *Shirley* on the subject of the condition of women. In June 1848, *The Tenant of Wildfell Hall* was published by T C Newby who had unscrupulously advertised it in such a way as to imply that it had been written to the best of his belief by the author of *Wuthering Heights* and *Jane Eyre*. He had been told repeatedly that it was not so. He had offered the book on these terms to an American with whom Smith, Elder & Co. had already made an agreement for Charlotte's next novel. Smith, Elder & Co. wrote a heated letter of protest.[59]

On the late afternoon of the day the letter arrived, 7 July, Charlotte and Anne walked through a thunderstorm to the railway station to catch a train from Keighley to Leeds and then travelled by night train to London to walk into the thunderstorm that was continuing to erupt in the premises of Smith, Elder & Co. at No. 65 Cornhill.

They arrived at the Chapter Coffee House on Paternoster Row at eight o'clock the next morning, which was a Saturday. After breakfast they had a discussion as to what to do next. Walking to Smith, Elder & Co. the two authors from Haworth informed a clerk that they wished to see Mr George Smith.

In a letter to Martha Taylor, Charlotte told how Smith came out, and asked: 'Did you wish to see me, Ma'am?' 'Is it Mr Smith?' Charlotte asked. 'It is,' he replied. She then put his latest letter to her in his hand which had been sent, of course, to 'Currer Bell.' He looked at it and then at Charlotte twice and, when Charlotte laughed, it dawned on him who she was. Charlotte told him her real name was 'Miss Brontë'.[60] It was quite a moment in literary history.

Charlotte and Anne were then introduced to George Smith's publishing partner, William Smith-Williams, and the animated conversation that followed must have been like a true meeting of the waters. Charlotte had to hold back her publisher's immediate desire to show London society who the Bell brothers really were. She insisted that their identity must remain a secret.[61]

What ensued was a whirlwind of activity. The authors were taken to the Opera House to see a performance of Rossini's *Barber of Seville.* Overwhelmed at the architecture and grandeur around them, Charlotte whispered to George Smith as she ascended the flight of stairs leading them from the grand entrance up to the lobby of the first tier of boxes: 'You know that I am not accustomed to this sort of thing.'[62]

The next morning they went to church at St Stephens, Walbrook, and then went to dine at George Smith's beautiful residence in Westbourne Place, Paddington. Monday saw them going round the exhibitions at the Royal Academy and the National Gallery on their own. If the people around them had realised who they really were they would not have been on their own for long. They spent the evening at William Smith-William's home and next morning, ladened with books given to them by George Smith, they left London and got safely home. They were exhausted.[63] Charlotte commented that 'a more jaded wretch than I looked, it would be difficult to conceive. I was weak, and yet restless.'[64]

Much to the author's delight, Smith, Elder & Co. now bought up the remainder of the *Poems* Edition from Aylott and Jones and prepared to reissue it. A whole new world had opened. The obscure but passionate daughters from Haworth parsonage who, as Charlotte put it once to Smith-Williams, 'lived like door-mice', were coming out into literary fame and sunshine.[65] It was not to last long for the darkest of all clouds, those of tragedy, now began to obliterate their joy.

TEN

Unrecognised Heather

'AFFLICTION,' CHARLOTTE wrote on reflection, 'came in that shape which to anticipate is dread; to look back on, grief.'[1] That affliction came to the gifted family living at Haworth parsonage time and again in the form of tuberculosis. It now moved in with a vengeance on Branwell. Other illnesses had disguised its approach.

Branwell's habits, of course, were also destroying him. 'He took opium,' writes Mrs Gaskell, 'because it made him forget for a time more effectually than drink; and, besides, it was more portable. In procuring it he showed all the cunning of the opium-eater. He would steal out while the family were at church – to which he had professed himself too ill to go – and manage to cajole the village druggist out of a lump; or, it might be, the carrier had unsuspiciously brought him some in a packet from a distance. For some time before his death he had attacks of *delirium tremens* of the most frightful character; he slept in his father's room, and he would sometimes declare that either he or his father should be dead before morning. The trembling sisters, sick with fright, would implore their father not to expose himself to this danger; but Mr Brontë is no timid man and, perhaps, he felt he could possibly influence his son to some self-restraint, more by showing trust in him than by showing fear.

'The sisters often listened for the report of a pistol in the dead of night, till watchful eye and hearkening ear grew heavy and dull with the perpetual strain upon their nerves. In the mornings young Brontë would saunter out, saying, with a drunkard's incontinence of speech, "The poor old man and I have had a terrible night of it; he does his best – the poor old man! but it's all over with me;" (whimpering) "it's *her* fault, *her* fault."'[2]

The death of Branwell Brontë has got to be one of the saddest of deaths. A former colleague from his days on the railway described inviting Branwell for dinner in a private room at the *Black Bull* in Haworth. Branwell was days away from death and Francis Grundy was deeply shocked by the sunken-eyed, gaunt, virtually insane man who turned up with his lips shaking. He was even more shocked when, on taking his leave, Branwell produced a carving knife from his sleeve, confessing that since he had not expected to see Grundy again he had imagined Satan had sent him the invitation to go to the *Black Bull*. Branwell had fully intended to rush into the room and stab its occupant. Only Grundy's voice had brought him back to his senses. A murder was, in fact, narrowly averted. The two friends parted with Branwell heart-breakingly standing in the road weeping.[3]

From Charlotte, in a letter to W S Williams, we learn that on Saturday 23 September 1848 when Branwell was unable to get out of his bed, the doctor was called. Dr Wheelhouse informed the family that Branwell was close to death. Patrick knelt by his bedside in prayer and begged his son to seek the salvation of his soul. Branwell was helped by his father to repentance of his sins. As he lay dying on his last night on earth, Branwell spoke of his 'misspent life, his wasted youth and his shame, with compunction.' When left alone with his friend, John Brown, he seized his hand, and cried: 'Oh, John, I am dying!' and then murmured, 'In all my past life I have done nothing either great or good.'[4]

On the following morning, all of Branwell's family were gathered around his bed as he approached death. In a letter to W S Williams, Charlotte wrote: 'I myself, with painful, mournful joy, heard him praying softly in his dying moments; and to the last prayer which my father offered up at his bedside, he added "Amen." How unusual that word appeared from his lips, of course you, who did not know him, cannot conceive. Akin to this alteration was that in his feelings towards his relations, all bitterness seemed gone.'[5] After a twenty-minute struggle, he died.

Charlotte mourned 'the wreck of talent, the ruin of promise, the untimely dreary extinction of what might have been a burning and a shining light.'[6] She wrote that her father 'naturally thought more of his *only* son than of his daughters, and, much and long as he had suffered on his account, he cried out for his loss like David for that of Absalom – "My son! My son!" – and refused to be comforted.'[7] Brontë readers across succeeding generations have also mourned the tragic life of Branwell Brontë and also felt deep sympathy for those who had to bear the consequences. He was a gifted man who had, tragically, lost his way.

Branwell was buried on 28 September 1847 in the family vault. His funeral service was taken by his godfather, the Rev William Morgan. What were his carefully chosen words on that

mournful day of wasted life and talent?[8] The Scriptures warn
that if we sow to the flesh we will reap the flesh and if we sow to
the Spirit we will reap the Spirit. Branwell had horrendously
reaped what he had sowed. We are not his ultimate judge but
his life is a warning beacon reaching far into a modern
generation where the temptation to sow to the flesh is every bit
as potent.

Autumn now brought a bitterly cold east wind across the
moors and around the parsonage at Haworth. Charlotte, who
had been unwell following the death of her brother, now began
to fear for her sister. By the end of October 1848, she began to
suspect that Emily had a pain in her chest and noticed a
shortness in her breathing when she moved at all quickly.

When anyone asked Emily a question about her health, she
refused to answer. When any remedies were recommended, she
refused to take them. Drawing on her faith, Charlotte said she
had to leave all in God's hands and to trust in his goodness but
admitted that 'faith and resignation are difficult to practise
under some circumstances.' She admitted to experiencing very
real depression at times. 'These things,' she wrote, 'make one
feel, as well as *know,* that this world is not our abiding place.
We should not knit human ties too close, or clasp affections too
fondly. They must leave us, or we must leave them, one day.
God restore health and strength to all who need it.'[9]

Emily faced her declining health with defiance, refusing to
see a doctor. She insisted in performing her usual domestic
duties, even though her pulse, the only time she allowed it to be
felt, was found to beat 115 per minute.[10]

Patrick who had, of course, already endured the death of
three of his children to tuberculosis was once more resigned to
the inevitability of Emily's death than he was to Charlotte and
Anne's cherishing of hope that she would survive.

The harrowing, dreary days at the parsonage were not helped by the arrival of Branwell's former lover's daughters, Mary, now Mrs Henry Clapham and Lydia on a visit.[11] Their mother had by now married Sir Edward Scott, whom she had pursued even as his wife was dying.[12] Mary and Lydia were delighted to meet up with their governess once more, but their arrival only exasperated the painful memory of Branwell's relationship with their mother.[13]

Affliction also circled the Brontë family at this time in the form of literary critics. Had they only realised their words were being read with amused scorn by the three women whom most critics thought were three men; had they only realised that death was about to take two of them in very quick succession, would they have written what they did? How quick the critic is to put in his or her barbed words. A short meditation on this practice is salutary.

Take John Keats, arguably the greatest romantic poet in English literature who died at twenty-six years of age. He left for us poems that haunt and touch the spirit as few other poets have done. Did he get much encouragement to do so in his lifetime? Try a *Blackwood's Magazine* review of his work: 'Mr Keats ... is only a boy of petty abilities which he has done everything in his power to spoil ... we venture to make one small prophecy, that his bookseller will not a second time venture fifty pounds sterling upon anything he can write. Is it a better and a wiser thing to be a starved chemist than a starved poet: so back to the shop, Mr John, back to plasters, pills and ointment boxes.' He died three years later. Were *Blackwood's Magazine* sorry? They said: 'A Mr John Keats ... has lately died of consumption, after having written two or three little books of verses, much neglected by the public. His vanity was probably wrung not less than his purse.'[14]

Twenty-seven years later, an account of Keats' life and works was published. Thomas Carlyle reviewed it. He wrote four words, calling the work: 'Fricassee of dead dog.'[15]

A little poem was once passed on to this author by William McLaughlin and it is poignantly relevant at this point to the lives of 'Currer, Ellis and Acton Bell'.

If with pleasure you are viewing,
Any work a man is doing,
If you like him or you love him, tell him now;
Don't withhold your approbation,
Till the Parson makes oration
And he lies with snow-white lilies on his brow.

For no matter how you shout it,
He won't really care about it,
He won't know how many teardrops you have shed;
If you think some praise is due him,
Now's the time to slip it to him,
For he cannot read his tombstone when he's dead.

More than fame and more than money,
Is the comment kind and sunny,
And the hearty warm approval of a friend;
For it gives to life a savour,
And it makes you stronger, braver,
And it gives you heart and spirit to the end.

If he earns your praise – bestow it,
If you like him, let him know it,
Let the words of true encouragement be said;
Do not wait till life is over,
And he's underneath the clover,
For he cannot read his tombstone when he's dead.

Would that one outstanding literary critic in the British Isles who had appreciated the works of particularly 'Acton and Ellis Bell' had spoken up at this time with unqualified praise because the 'Parson' would soon make oration across their graves. That outstanding critic's encouragement was not to be read by either author at the Brontë parsonage. *The Tenant of Wildfell Hall* and *Wuthering Heights* were, in general, damned as 'coarse' and 'brutal' novels.

No writer's words could ever quite capture the death of Emily Brontë better than those of her heartbroken sister, Charlotte. She wrote: 'Neither Ellis nor Acton allowed herself for one moment to sink under want of encouragement; energy nerved the one, and endurance upheld the other. They were both prepared to try again; I would fain think that hope and the sense of power was yet strong within them. But a great change approached: affliction came in that shape which to anticipate is dread; to look back on, grief. In the very heat and burden of the day, the labourers failed over their work.

'My sister, Emily, first declined. The details of her illness are deep branded in my memory, but to dwell on them, either in thought or narrative, is not in my power. Never in all her life had she lingered over any task that lay before her, and she did not linger now. She sank rapidly. She made haste to leave us. Yet, while physically she perished, mentally she grew stronger than we had yet known her. Day by day, when I saw with what a front she met suffering, I looked on her with an anguish of wonder and love. I have seen nothing like it; but, indeed, I have never seen her parallel in anything. Stronger than a man, simpler than a child, her nature stood alone. The awful point was, that while full of ruth for others, on herself she had no pity; the spirit was inexorable to the flesh; from the trembling hand, the unnerved limbs, the faded eyes, the same service was exacted as they had rendered in health. To stand by and witness this, and not dare to remonstrate, was a pain no words can render.

'Two cruel months of hope and fear passed painfully by, and the day came at last when the terrors and pains of death were to be undergone by this treasure, which had grown dearer and dearer to our hearts as it wasted before our eyes.'[16]

It is harrowing to learn that Charlotte went out across the moors in that December of 1848 to search in the little borders and sheltered crevices for 'a lingering spray of heather', however withered, to give to Emily. She found one and was pained to realise that 'the flower was not recognised by the dim and indifferent eyes.'[17]

On the day she died, Tuesday 19 December, Emily rose and slowly dressed herself as usual. When she eventually got downstairs she took up her sewing. Her rattling breath and glazed eyes told that she was dying but she sewed on. 'The morning drew on to noon, Emily was worse: she could only whisper on gasps. Now, when it was too late, she said to Charlotte, "If you will send for a doctor, I will see him now."'[18] About two o'clock she died in the arms of her family. She was thirty years of age.

It was a pitiful scene 'as the old, bereaved father and his two surviving children followed the coffin to the grave. They were joined by Keeper, Emily's fierce, faithful bulldog. He walked alongside of the mourners and into the church, and stayed quietly there all the time as the burial service was being read. When he came home, he lay down at Emily's chamber door, and howled pitifully for many days. Anne Brontë drooped and sickened more rapidly from that time; and so ended the year 1848.'[19] It must have been, of all the Christmas seasons in the Brontë family, the bleakest to date.

The New Year brought Anne's swift decline. Outwardly patient and gentle in the face of the onslaught of tuberculosis,

Anne, unlike Emily, submitted to all medicines proffered by her doctors. When her father called in Mr Teale, a specialist from Leeds, he confirmed to Patrick after examining Anne that she was already in the advanced stages of tuberculosis. After he departed, Patrick drew Anne towards him, and said: 'My *dear* little Anne.'[20] That simple action confirmed the imminence of Anne's death.

In April 1848 Anne composed her final poem. In a previous poem, *Music on Christmas Morning*, written from the experience of hearing the Christmas bells ring from her father's church, she wrote:

> *While listening to that sacred strain,*
> *My raptured spirit soars on high;*
> *I seem to hear those songs again*
> *Resounding through the open sky,*
> *That kindled such divine delight,*
> *In those who watched their flocks by night.*

> *With them, I celebrate his birth –*
> *Glory to God, in highest Heaven,*
> *Goodwill to men and peace on Earth,*
> *To us a Saviour-king is given;*
> *Our God is come to claim his own,*
> *And Satan's power is overthrown!*

> *Now holy Peace may smile from Heaven,*
> *And heavenly Truth from earth shall spring:*
> *The captive's galling bonds are riven,*
> *For our Redeemer is our king;*
> *And he that gave his blood for men*
> *Will lead us home to God again.*[21]

The turmoil in Anne's deepest soul surfaces, though, in her final poem written after Mr Teale's visit. Her faith fights to calm the Tempter's whispers:

A dreadful darkness closes in
On my bewildered mind
O, let me suffer and not sin,
Be tortured, yet resigned.

Through all this world of whirling mist,
Still let me look to thee
And give me courage to resist
The Tempter till he flee.

The overwhelming theme of the poem is that the opportunity to carry on her work, motivated by the keen and high purpose of glorifying God in every part of her identity has been taken away. Now that she knows that she is dying, Anne realises, as we all need to realise, that her life was on loan. She feels that she has not been grateful enough for what she had:

O, thou hast taken my delight,
And hope of life away
And bid me watch the painful night,
And wait the weary day.

The hope and the delight were thine,
I bless thee for their loan
I gave thee while I deemed them mine
Too little thanks I own.[22]

Her faith now rose to help her find meaning in her suffering; her words are brave, beautiful and humble, signalling that acceptance of her destiny had brought peace:

These weary hours will not be lost,
These days of passive misery,
These nights of darkness anguish-tossed,
If I can fix my heart on Thee...

...That secret labour to sustain,
With humble patience every blow
To gather fortitude from Pain,
And hope and holiness from Woe.

Thus let me serve thee from my heart,
Whate'er my written fate
Whether thus early to depart,
Or yet awhile to wait.

If Thou shoulds't bring me back to life,
More humbled I should be
More Wise more strengthened for the strife,
More apt to lean on Thee.

Should Death be standing at the gate,
Thus should I keep my vow
But Lord whate'er my future fate,
So let me serve thee now. [23]

Anne rallied a little at the end of January and Charlotte now submitted the first volume of her new book, *Shirley*, to Smith,

Elder & Co. pleading for honest criticism. Two criticisms emerged: one was that her male characters were not as impressive as her female characters, another was that the first chapter with its vitriolic observations on clerics was not artistic enough. Charlotte agreed to the first criticism and dug her heels in on the second.[24]

Death, though, as ever, now moved in again on the Brontë household. 'I have, indeed, had my ample share of trouble,' Patrick wrote to a friend, 'but it has been the Lord's will ... my only son has died, and soon after him, a beloved daughter died also − for these things we may weep, since Christ himself wept over his dead friend ... yet, whilst we grieve, it should not be without hope.' He sent his kind regards from 'all my family that remain.'[25]

In March, Anne was kindly invited to stay with Ellen Nussey. Ellen was seeking to relieve Charlotte of the great burden of nursing Anne and proposed that she and her sisters look after her. Anne, while appreciating Ellen's offer, declined, not wishing to impose herself on an already overcrowded household. She then asked, through Charlotte, if Ellen would accompany her to an inland watering place or to the seaside on the doctor's recommendation.[26] Charlotte and Patrick were not happy about her proposal but when the specialist, Mr Teale, had no objections, they relented.[27] Patrick was never to see his Anne on earth again.

Anne, Charlotte and Ellen travelled to Scarborough via York. Due to Anne's weakness, she used a bath chair to get out and about and Mrs Gaskell notes through Charlotte that 'the dear invalid was so revived, so cheerful and so happy' that Charlotte and Ellen 'drew consolation and trusted that at least temporary improvement was to be derived from the change which *she* had longed for, and her friends had so dreaded for her.'[28]

At Anne's request she was taken to York Minster and a poignant proof of her spirituality emerged. One of the finest gothic cathedrals in the world, its open spaces, peaceful chapels and beautiful stain glass windows make it one of Britain's most famous buildings. The height from floor to vault is over 27 metres. Its twin west towers are about 56 metres high. The lantern tower is 71 metres. York Minster was built between the 12th and 15th century and, today, two million people every year make a visit.[29] As Anne Brontë gazed up at the cathedral's grandeur on Saturday 25 May 1849, Charlotte recorded that 'to her it was overpowering pleasure; not for its own imposing and impressive grandeur only, but because it brought to her susceptible nature a vital and overwhelming sense of omnipotence. She said, while gazing at the structure: "If finite power can do this, what is the ...?" and, here, emotion stayed her speech, and she was hastened to a less exciting scene.

'Her weakness of body was great, but her attitude for every mercy was greater. After such exertion as walking to her bedroom, she would clasp her hands and raise her eyes in silent thanks, and she did this not to the exclusion of wonted prayer, for that too was performed on bended knee, ere she accepted the rest of her couch.'[30]

Rooms had been taken in Scarborough at Woods Lodgings at No. 2 The Cliff with a good-sized sitting room and an airy double-bedded room both commanding a sea view. It was one of the best situations in the town.[31]

The day after arrival at Scarborough, Saturday 26 May, found the emaciated Anne with her arms no thicker than a child's and with impeded breath, insisting on going to the baths and being left there alone with only the attendant in charge. She walked back to the lodgings alone and collapsed at the garden gate. Charlotte and Ellen only found out later about her accident.

The afternoon found her driving herself for an hour on the sands in a donkey cart, 'lest the poor donkey should be urged by its driver to a greater speed than her tender heart thought right.' When joined by Ellen she was found charging the donkey's boy master to treat the animal well.[32]

Anne passionately wanted to attend morning worship at a local church on Sunday 27 May, but was dissuaded by Charlotte and Ellen. In the afternoon she walked a little, finding a comfortable and sheltered seat near the beach. She insisted that Ellen and Charlotte would leave her to explore the scenes near at hand. Anne Brontë enjoyed her final view of an earthly sunset that evening.

The pathos of that achingly beautiful sunset is best described by Charlotte: 'The evening closed in with the most glorious sunset ever witnessed. The castle on the cliff stood in proud glory gilded by the rays of the declining sun. The distant ships glittered like burnished gold; the little boats near the beach heaved on the ebbing tide. The view was grand beyond description. Anne was drawn in her easy chair to the window, to enjoy the scene with us. Her face became illumined almost as much as the glorious scene she gazed upon. Little was said, for it was plain that her thoughts were driven by the imposing view before her to penetrate forwards to the regions of unfading glory. She again thought of public worship, and wished us to leave her, and join those who were assembled at the House of God. We declined, gently urging the duty and pleasure of staying with her, who was now so dear and so feeble. On returning to her place near the fire, she conversed with her sister upon the propriety of returning to their home. She did not wish it for her own sake, she said; she was fearing others might suffer more if her decease occurred where she was. She probably thought the task of accompanying her lifeless remains on a long journey was more than her sister could bear – more than the bereaved father could bear, were she borne home another, and a third tenant of the family-vault in the short space of nine months.'[33]

Anne rose at seven o'clock the next morning and, unable to descend the stairs because of faintness, Ellen carried her down to an easy chair. During the process, Anne's head fell like a leaden weight on Ellen's and Ellen thought Anne had died. Anne then put out her arms to comfort her much distressed friend.[34]

About 11.00am Anne took a turn for the worse and asked could she reach home alive if they left immediately? Charlotte sent for a doctor and Anne, with perfect composure, begged him to tell her how long she thought she might live. She told him not to fear telling the truth for she was not afraid to die.

'The doctor reluctantly admitted that the angel of death was already arrived, and that life was ebbing fast.' Anne thanked him for his truthfulness and he departed, promising to return again soon.

Looking serene and reliant, Anne now clasped her hands and 'reverently invoked a blessing from on high; first upon her sister and then upon her friend, to whom she said, "Be a sister in my stead. Give Charlotte as much of your company as you can,"' thanking both of them for their kindness and attention.

Now getting restless as death approached, Anne was carried to a sofa and 'on being asked if she were easier, she looked gratefully at her questioner, and said: "It is not *you* who can give me ease, but soon all will be well, through the merits of our Redeemer."' Seeing Charlotte now fighting hard to restrain her almost overwhelming grief, Anne looked at her, and said: 'Take courage, Charlotte; take courage.'

Charlotte described what happened. 'Her faith never failed, and her eye never dimmed till about two o'clock, when she calmly and without a sigh passed from the temporal to the eternal. So still, and so hallowed were her last hours and moments.'[35] She was twenty-nine-years-old.

So quickly had Anne died, the uninformed hostess announced dinner through the half-opened door just as Charlotte was closing Anne's eyes. The doctor who had returned several times during Anne's final hours later testified that he had never witnessed such a death bed scene and wondered at Anne's 'fixed tranquillity of spirit and longing to be gone.'[36]

The tide of grief now burst on Charlotte and it was not until the next day that she could gather her thoughts and make arrangements for Anne's interment in Scarborough. Charlotte decided to have the funeral service quickly to spare her father the agony of having to attend the funeral of his third child in nine months. She also wished to spare him a harrowing and long journey to Scarborough. She wrote immediately to inform him of the plans.

Anne Brontë's funeral service was held at Christ Church, Scarborough on Wednesday 30 May 1849 and she was buried in the cemetery of St Mary's, Scarborough facing the sea and just below Scarborough Castle, as Charlotte put it:

Where the south sun warms the now dear sod,
Where the ocean billows lave and strike the steep and turf-covered rock.[37]

Patrick, with further indication of his loving nature towards his children, now wrote to his last grieving daughter telling her to stay a while longer by the seaside. It was, by any standards, a remarkably gracious letter, seeing that he had been given no chance of stating where Anne should be buried and had not been consulted regarding his wishes about whether or not he should attend her funeral service. His letter exemplified grace under indescribable pressure. To be fair to Charlotte, she could well have thought that the journey to and attendance at Anne's funeral service might well have killed him.[38]

Charlotte decided to move down the East Coast about ten miles to the Yorkshire resort of Filey with Ellen and then spent a few days with friends at Bridlington.[39] She arrived home at Haworth on 20 June.

How did she feel? Her father and the servants awaited her and received her with affection. When, eventually, Charlotte entered the dining room and shut the door she had the sensation of the feeling of a silent house with empty rooms. She wrote of 'feeling confidence in [God] who has upheld me hitherto.' She admitted as the days passed that her greatest trial came when the evenings closed in. She would remember how her family would assemble in the dining room and talk. She now sat by herself, silently.[40]

Writing to Ellen on 14 July 1849, Charlotte poured out her feelings about the future: 'My life is what I expected it to be. Sometimes when I wake in the morning, and know that Solitude, Remembrance and Longing are to be almost my sole companions all day through, that at night I shall go to bed with them, that they will long keep me sleepless, that next morning I shall wake to them again; sometimes, Nell, I have a heavy heart of it. But crushed I am not, yet; nor robbed of elasticity, nor of hope, nor quite of endeavour. I have some strength to fight the battle of life. I am aware, and can acknowledge, I have many comforts, many mercies. Still I can *get on*. But I do hope and pray, that never may you, or any one I love, be placed as I am. To sit in a lonely room, the clock ticking loud through a still

house, and have open before the mind's eye the record of the last
year, with its shocks, sufferings and losses is a trial. I write to
you freely, because I believe you will hear me with moderation –
that you will not take alarm or think me in any way worse off
than I am.'[41]

How would she, though, '*get on*'? Mercifully, she lifted her
pen again.

ELEVEN

That Woman Was a Manager

IF CHARLOTTE had been lonely in Brussels, her loneliness in Haworth now that her family had been virtually decimated, was of a very different kind. She now turned again to her novel *Shirley* but this time there were no sisters to pace the dining room floor in the evenings; there was no one to whom she could read her tale or with whom she could discuss it. There was nobody to criticise a line or commend a paragraph. She listened for echoing steps that never came and heard 'the wind sobbing at the window, with an almost inarticulate sound.'[1]

Patrick had another attack of bronchitis and Charlotte, well aware that he was the last of her near family left in the world, felt very uneasy. Happily, the illness was temporary. Every sign of illness in her own body filled her with trepidation. She had continually recurring feelings of slight cold and slight soreness in the throat and chest.[2]   Charlotte's writing was now to be deeply affected by the trauma of what she had experienced. She told Mrs Gaskell that the first chapter of *Shirley,* written after Anne's death, was the one entitled, The Valley of the Shadow.[3]

Only a heart that had experienced grief could express the words spoken by Catherine Helstone's mother by the bedside of her daughter who was near death: 'Oh, child! the human heart can suffer. It can hold more tears than the ocean holds waters. We may never know how deep, how wide it is, till misery begins to unbind her clouds, and fill it with rushing blackness.'

It was an experienced mind that wrote the haunting first paragraph to the chapter: 'The future sometimes seems to sob a low warning of the events it is bringing us, like some gathering though yet remote storm, which, in tones of the wind, in flushings of the firmament, in clouds strangely torn, announces a blast strong to strew the sea with wrecks; or commissioned to bring in fog the yellow taint of pestilence, covering white Western isles with the poisoned exhalations of the East, dimming the lattices of English homes with the breath of Indian plague. At other times this Future bursts suddenly, as if a rock had rent, and in it a grave had opened, whence issues the body of one that slept. Ere you are aware, you stand face to face with a shrouded and unthought-of Calamity – a new Lazarus.'

It was from the experience of what she had recently witnessed that Charlotte could write of Caroline Helstone: 'She wasted like any snow-wreath in thaw; she faded like any flower in drought.'

As the winds howled around the Haworth parsonage as the desperately lonely Charlotte wrote her novel, she is surely musing on her sister's recent death when she makes Caroline Helstone muse on her after-life: 'What can my departed soul feel then? Can it see or know what happens to the clay? Can spirits, through any medium, communicate with living flesh? Can the dead at all revisit those they leave? Can they come in the elements? Will wind, water, fire, lend me a path to Moore? ... *Where* is the other world? In *what* will another life consist? Who do I ask? Have I not cause to think that the hour is hasting but too fast when the veil must be rent for me? Do I not know the Grand Mystery is likely to burst prematurely on me? Great Spirit! in whose goodness I confide; whom, as my Father, I have petitioned night and morning from early infancy, help the weak creation of thy hands! Sustain me through the ordeal I dread and must undergo! Give me strength! Give me patience! Give me – oh! *give me* FAITH!'

Charlotte describes Catherine's mother's prayers throughout the critical evening of Catherine's hovering near death as being like Jacob at Peniel: 'Till break of day, she wrestled with God in earnest prayer.'[4]

How haunting are the lines in the following chapter of *Shirley*, entitled, The West Wind Blows: 'Not always do those who dare such divine conflict prevail. Night after night the sweat of agony may burst dark on the forehead; the supplicant may cry for mercy with that soundless voice the soul utters when its appeal is to the Invisible. "Spare my beloved," it may implore. "Heal my life's life. Rend not from me what long affection entwines with my whole nature. God of heaven, bend, hear, be clement!" And after this cry and strife, the sun may rise and see him worsted.'

In this case, though, Charlotte allows Caroline Helston to live. What must her own heart and mind have felt and thought as she wrote the following words: 'So long as the breath of Asiatic deserts parched Caroline's lips and fevered her veins, her physical convalescence could not keep pace with her returning mental tranquillity: but there came a day when the wind ceased to sob at the eastern gable of the rectory, and at the oriel window of the church. A little cloud like a man's hand arose in the west; gusts from the same quarter drove it on and spread it wide; wet and tempest prevailed awhile. When that was over the sun broke out genially, heaven regained its azure, and earth its green; the livid cholera-tint had vanished from the face of nature: the hills rose clear round the horizon, absolved from that pale malaria-haze.'[5]

Shirley was ready to go to the publishers in August 1849. The manuscript was picked up in Haworth on 8 September by a subordinate member of Smith, Elder & Co., a red-haired Scotsman called James Taylor. While her publishers were genuinely favourable to the book, they outright rejected her preface. Stung by a critic of *Jane Eyre* called Elizabeth Rigby in the *Quarterly Review* of December 1848, Charlotte had risen to attack her with stinging sarcasm in her preface to *Shirley*. That Rigby had also propagated the false story that the author of *Jane Eyre* had been Thackeray's governess had not helped things.

Her postscript lashed out: 'I read all you said about governesses. My dear Madam, just turn out and be a governess yourself for a couple of years, the experiment would do you good; a little irksome toil, a little unpitied suffering, two years of uncheered solitude might perhaps teach you that to be callous, harsh and unsympathising is not to be firm, superior and magnanimous.'[6]

As the publication of *Shirley* neared, Smith, Elder & Co. now tried to persuade Charlotte to give up her pseudonym; the whole question of her identity was becoming a matter for a lot of speculation and comment and they were keen to unveil the true Currer Bell to a fascinated public. Charlotte was not keen.

On 21 September she wrote to W S Williams: 'I am obliged to

you for preserving my secret, being at least as anxious as ever (*more* anxious I cannot well be) to keep quiet. You asked me in one of your letters lately, whether I thought I should escape identification in Yorkshire, I am so little known that I think I shall. Besides, the book is far less founded on the Real, than perhaps appears. It would be difficult to explain to you how little actual experience I have had of life, how few persons I have known, and how very few have known me.'[7]

The truth was, though, that Charlotte was not going to be able to hide much longer. It was Joe Taylor who eventually let Charlotte's secret out. Charlotte sent him copies of the chapters in which the Taylor family had appeared as the Yorke's in *Shirley*. Joe kindly remarked that Charlotte had not drawn himself and his family strong enough![8]

The novel was published on 26 October 1848 and most critics were agreed that the novel proved the author was, in fact, a woman. They were also highly critical of the structure, plot and unity of the novel which they saw 'badly wanting.' David Harrison has succinctly summed up the criticisms of the novel. He points out that there are a number of hugely interesting stories in the work, 'each one of which might have been developed into a successful plot had the author taken the time or trouble to develop them separately. Had Charlotte focused on one theme or element and developed it fully with time, consideration and effort, *Shirley* could have been much closer to the quality and success of *Jane Eyre*.'[9]

Is *Shirley* a romantic novel? Is it a social commentary on selected topics? Is it a historical novel based on the Luddite riots of the early 1800s? The fact that Charlotte changed the title of the novel from *Hollows Mill* to *Fieldhead* and then to *Shirley* shows Charlotte's own indecisiveness regarding its direction and theme.[10]

None of this criticism, though, can hide the fact that Charlotte's genius shines through at times. The first chapter is an example. Her publishers had not liked it and wanted it removed, but Charlotte dug her heels in. She refused to remove it, arguing that it was based on the truth.[11] Charles Kingsley, author of *Westward Ho* and the *Water Babies*, was so disgusted with the chapter that he gave up reading Charlotte's books because he considered her a person who liked coarseness. He later, wisely, changed his misconceptions of Charlotte and said that she was a whole heaven above him.[12]

The three curates, the Revs Donne, Malone and Sweeting, are portrayed in the chapter as wasting their time visiting one another instead of attending to their pastoral duties. They are pilloried for senseless quarrelling and lack of spirituality. Status is more important to them than matters of faith or the application of Christian truth and living. It is worth highlighting that Charlotte's pillorying of these three curates is later balanced in the final chapter of the book entitled, Winding Up.

The life of the boisterous Irishman, the Rev Malone, is dismissed as 'catastrophic' but it is mainly blamed on his inability to realise that parishioners don't like being told the simple truth. Charlotte's paragraph finally addressing the Rev Peter Malone is a most incredible example of her writing genius: 'Whenever you present the actual, simple truth, it is, somehow, always denounced as a lie: they disown it, cast if off, throw it on the parish; whereas the product of your own imagination, the mere figment, the sheer fiction, is adopted, petted, termed pretty, proper, sweetly natural: the little spurious wretch gets all the comfits – the honest, lawful bantling all the cuffs. Such is the way of the world, Peter; and, as you are the legitimate urchin, rude, unwashed, and naughty, you must stand down.'

As for the Rev Sweeting, he is dismissed with a comfortable living and a wealthy wife who is 'the weightiest woman in Yorkshire'. 'They lived,' we are told, 'long and happily together, beloved by their parishioners and by a numerous circle of friends.' 'There,' adds the author, 'I think the varnish has been put on very nicely.'

The Rev Donne is also dismissed with a comfortable marriage. Famous for his fundraising, 'when Mr Donne set out on begging expeditions, he armed himself in a complete suit of brazen mail; that you had given a hundred pounds yesterday, was, with him, no reason why you should not give two hundred today; he would tell you so to your face, and, ten to one, get the money out of you; people gave to get rid of him. After all, he did some good with the cash; he was useful in his day and generation.'

Charlotte, though, saw through it all to the heart of what she felt a pastor should be about, namely, pastoring people's souls. 'As a pastor,' she wrote, 'he, to his dying day, conscientiously refused to act.' She then began to draw on Christ's powerful exposure of hypocrisy in religious leaders when he likened them to whitewashed tombs, beautiful on the outside but full of dead men's bones on the inside, appearing outwardly righteous but inwardly full of hypocrisy (Matthew 23:27-28).

Writing of the Rev Donne, she commented: 'The outside of the cup and platter he burnished up with the best polishing-powder; the furniture of the altar and temple he looked after with the zeal of an upholsterer, the care of a cabinet-maker. His little school, his little church, his little parsonage, all owed their erection to him, and they did him credit; each was a model in its way. If uniformity and taste in architecture had been the same thing as consistency and earnestness in religion, what a shepherd of a Christian flock Mr Donne would have made!'

While the Rev Peter Malone is based on the character and life of the Rev James Smith, one of Patrick's former curates, Charlotte also, intriguingly, wrote of Patrick's present curate, the Rev Arthur Bell Nicholls. It was written five years before her marriage to him and she places him in *Shirley* in the form of the Rev Malone's replacement, the Rev Macarthey. Ah! love grows in rare places!

She wrote: 'Perhaps I ought to remark that, on the premature and sudden vanishing of Mr Malone from the stage of Briarfield parish (you cannot know how it happened, reader; your curiosity must be robbed to pay your elegant love of the pretty and pleasing), there came as his successor another Irish curate, Mr Macarthey. I am happy to be able to inform you, *with truth,* that this gentleman did as much credit to his country as Malone had done it discredit: he proved himself as decent, decorous and conscientious, as Peter was rampant, boisterous, and - (this last epithet I choose to suppress, because it would let the cat out of the bag). He laboured faithfully in the parish: the schools, both Sunday and day-schools, flourished under his sway like green bay-trees.

'Being human, of course, he had his faults; these, however, were proper, steady-going, clerical faults; what many would call virtues: the circumstance of finding himself invited to tea with a dissenter would unhinge him for a week; the spectacle of a Quaker wearing his hat in the church, the thought of an unbaptised fellow-creature being interred with Christian rites – these things could make strange havoc in Mr Macarthey's physical and mental economy; otherwise he was sane and rational, diligent and charitable.'[13]

It is important to note that the Rev Nicholls, Charlotte informed Ellen Nussey, found *Shirley* delightful and gave vent to roars of laughter as he sat reading the novel, clapping his hands and stamping on the floor. He would read all the scenes about the curates aloud to Patrick and, said Charlotte, 'he triumphed in his own character' in the novel![14]

Charlotte characterised in the novel other clergyman she had known, namely the Rev Hammond Roberson, since deceased, as the Rev Helstone and the Rev W M Heald, vicar of Birstall, as the Rev Hall.

Soon, of course, their parishioners recognised the characterisation of their curates and the setting of the novel in the communities of Birstall and Gomersal. People in the area began to suspect that 'Currer Bell' was, indeed, Charlotte Brontë.

No study of *Shirley* should leave out the powerful plea Charlotte makes for feminism, particularly Christian feminism. Caroline Helstone, living within the confines of her uncle's rectory, is deeply frustrated by its strictures. Her mindset is opened up for the reader: 'I believe single women should have more to do, better chances of interesting and profitable occupation than they possess now. And when I speak thus, I have no impression that I displease God by my words: that I am either impious or impatient, irreligious or sacrilegious. My consolation is, indeed, that God hears many a groan, and compassionates much grief which man stops his ears against, or frowns on with impotent contempt. I say *impotent,* for I observe that to such grievances as society cannot readily cure, it usually forbids utterance, on pain of its scorn: this scorn being only a sort of tinselled cloak to its deformed weakness.

'People hate to be reminded of ills they are unable or unwilling to remedy: such reminder, in forcing on them a sense of their own incapacity, or a more painful sense of an obligation to make some unpleasant effort, troubles their ease and shakes their self-complacency. Old maids, like the houseless and unemployed poor, should not ask for a place and an occupation in the world: the demand disturbs the happy and rich: it disturbs parents.

'Look at the numerous families of girls in this neighbourhood: The Armitages, the Birtwistles, the Sykes. The brothers of these girls are every one in business or in professions; they have something to do: their sisters have no earthly employment, but household work and sewing; no earthly pleasure, but an unprofitable visiting; and no hope, in all their life to come, of anything better. This stagnant state of things makes them decline in health: they are never well; and their minds and views shrink to wondrous narrowness. The great wish, the sole aim of every one of them is to be married, but the majority will never marry: they will die as they now live.'

Caroline emphasises that fathers expect their daughters to simply stay at home and sew and cook. She remarks that if fathers were forced to live such a life themselves: 'Would they not be very weary? And when there came no relief to their weariness, but only reproaches at its slightest manifestation, would not their weariness ferment in time to frenzy?'

Caroline also muses on the way that Solomon's virtuous woman of Proverbs 31 'is often quoted' as patterns of what 'the sex (as they say) ought to be.' She argues that this woman 'had something more to do than spin and give out portions: she was a manufacturer – she made fine linen and sold it: she was an agriculturist – she bought estates and planted vineyards. *That* woman was a manager ...'

Caroline likes Solomon's model, and writes: '"Strength and honour were her clothing: the heart of her husband safely trusted in her. She opened her mouth with wisdom; in her tongue was the law of kindness: her children rose up and called her blessed; her husband also praised her." King of Israel! your model of a woman is a worthy model! But are we, in these days, brought up to be like her? Men of Yorkshire! do your daughters reach this royal standard? Can they reach it? Can you help them to reach it? Can you give them a field in which their faculties may be exercised and grow? Men of England! look at your poor girls, many of them fading round you, dropping off in consumption or decline; or, what is worse, degenerating to sour old maids – envious, backbiting, wretched, because life is a desert to them: or, what is worst of all, reduced to strive, by scarce modest coquetry and debasing artifice, to gain that position and consideration by marriage, which to celibacy is denied. Fathers! cannot you alter these things? Perhaps not all at once; but consider the matter well when it is brought before you, receive it as a theme worthy of thought: do not dismiss it with an idle jest or an unmanly insult.

'You would wish to be proud of your daughters and not to blush for them – then seek for them an interest and an occupation which shall raise them above the flirt, the maneuverer, the mischief-making tale-bearer. Keep your girls' minds narrow and fettered – they will still be a plague and a care, sometimes a disgrace to you: cultivate them, give them scope and work – they will be your gayest companions in health; your tenderest nurses in sickness; your most faithful prop in age.'[15]

Let it not be said that Charlotte believed that marriage was the supreme answer to the problems faced by single women. A study of *Shirley* shows the futility of marriage without love. If only for the way the novel deals with the subjects of middle class single women and marriage alone, it deserves a significant place in the literature of the 19th century. The book, though, must have held a very special place in Charlotte's heart. She told Mrs Gaskell that *Shirley* herself was her representation of her sister

Emily. Charlotte tried to depict Emily's character in Shirley Keeldar 'as what Emily Brontë would have been, had she been placed in health and prosperity.'[16]

Anonymity for Charlotte Brontë was now being whittled away by the day and was not helped by George Lewes who had given 'Currer Bell' severe treatment in the *Edinburgh Review*. He had discovered Charlotte's identity from a former fellow pupil at the Cowan Bridge School[17] Bit by bit her identity leaked out and then reached the press.

Charlotte now decided it was time to go to London and publicly declare her identity. She was encouraged by George Smith, the young head of Smith, Elder & Co. who was helping her with the investment of the £500 she had received for *Shirley*.[18] She set off for London on 29 November 1849 to stay with George Smith and his mother and sisters in Westbourne Place in Paddington. Charlotte had left Haworth where the tick of the clock could be heard all day long for the world's greatest metropolis, once more.

Charlotte was taken to the theatre to see the famous actor William Macready in *Macbeth* and *Othello*,[19] met her hero Thackeray who spoke of her 'great honest eyes'[20] and the novelist and essayist Harriet Marineau who spoke of her as 'the smallest creature I have ever seen (except at a fair) and her eyes blazed.'[21] It was Thackeray who unveiled her identity to literary circles in London. Charlotte also had dinner with some leading literary critics, one of whom had made her cry with his review of *Shirley* in *The Times*. She met and conversed with them courageously and survived the experience with good grace despite the fact that they 'had done their best or worst' to write her down.[22] She returned to Haworth on 15 December.

As Christmas descended on Haworth it must have been a time of indescribable sadness. No season is more inclined to touch memory for families than Christmas and Patrick and Charlotte had family memories by the thousand to haunt them. Yet we find Patrick with his Christian faith strong and proving in his life the truth of the promise that, 'As your days so shall your strength be.'[23]

He lifted his pen in the darkness of his circumstances to hail the season which brought the Light of the World to earth. His Christmas hymn was published three days before Christmas 1849 in the *Leeds Intelligencer:*

Then welcome with pleasures profound
The joys which the season commands.
Let Christ and his love be our theme,
Let earth with its cares pass away,
Let heavenly thoughts be our dreams,
And practice our duty by day.[24]

For all his idiosyncrasies Patrick Brontë remained through all the storms of his life deeply faithful to his Christian calling and to the Lord who had called him. Lesser men would have buckled under the strain and turned to an easier life but Patrick, in the words of the idiom Christ used, put his hand to the plough and did not look back.[25]

Ellen Nussey came to stay with Charlotte for three weeks after Christmas and continued to prove to be the most faithful friend she ever had.[26] As news of Charlotte's authorship began to spread like wildfire, Ellen was truly proud of Charlotte's accomplishments and was happy to claim her close relationship with Charlotte in her hour of power. Soon Haworth was ablaze with the news of Charlotte's books and even Martha Brown, a servant at the parsonage, burst in upon Charlotte to tell her the news she had heard of her mistress having written 'two books – the grandest books that was ever seen!'[27]

Soon the *Bradford Observer* published the news of Charlotte's identity and her anonymity was gone forever.[28] She had put up a long and brave fight to preserve it but the battle was lost. Like it or not, Charlotte had become a nineteenth century celebrity.

Despite Charlotte's growing fame, an underlying depression constantly threatened her. Her father, in his old age, now retired to bed after 8.00pm prayers as did Tabby the servant, and the nights were long for Charlotte. The howling, sobbing winds around the parsonage were 'as of the dearly-beloved striving to force their way to her.' Her father was out on parish duties most of the day, leaving Charlotte alone with Tabby. Mrs Gaskell, in writing of this time in her biography of Charlotte, makes the point that 'the reader, who has even faintly pictured to himself her life at this time – the solitary days [and] the waking, watching nights – may imagine to what a sensitive pitch her nerves were strung, and how such a state was sure to affect her health.'[29]

Her father was well aware of the situation and was keen to ensure that Charlotte had a change of scenery and circumstance by urging her to get out of the house on another trip. He urged her to take up the invitation of Sir James Kay-Shuttleworth, the medical and educational reformer, and Lady Kay-Shuttleworth, to visit them at their castillated mansion, Gawthorpe Hall, Lancashire. Reluctantly, and particularly under pressure from her father, she went, and all in all enjoyed it. She returned home refreshed after 'quiet drives to old ruins and old halls, situated among older hills and woods' and was not exhausted by 'dialogues by the old fireside in the antique oak-panelled drawing-room.'[30]

Unfortunately, illness reared its ugly head once more and Charlotte caught a bad cold and had a recurring sore throat,

Martha Brown experienced fever and tic-doloureux and Patrick continued to be bronchitic.[31]

Yet, there must have been real pleasure for him when Haworth was at last visited in April by Benjamin Babbage, an inspector commissioned by the General Board of Health in London. He came to investigate the water supply and sanitary conditions in Haworth in response to a campaign by Patrick and others to have a better water supply. They believed the poor health conditions and high mortality rate in the town was due to bad sanitary conditions and lack of a supply of pure water. The inspector produced a damning report that recommended the installation of sewers, a piped water supply and at least one water closet for every three homes, the setting up of a public slaughterhouse and the immediate closure of the churchyard.[32] Let it never be said that Patrick Brontë was too heavenly-minded to be of any earthly use.

June 1850 found Charlotte in London again, urged on by her father whose health had improved, and invited by George Smith of Smith, Elder & Co. She stayed at the Smith's new home at No. 26 Gloucester Terrace in Hyde Park Gardens. It was back to the opera and the Royal Academy. There were also visits to the Zoological Gardens and even the Ladies' Gallery of the House of Commons. She visited the Chapel Royal and caught sight of her great hero, the Duke of Wellington. They followed the Duke out of the Chapel and George Smith so arranged their walk that they met him twice on his way back to his famous Piccadilly home, Apsley House. It is known as No. 1 London and is situated at Hyde Park Corner and is still, even in the 21st century, an amazing place to visit.[33]

Charlotte had two further meetings with Thackeray, one of them at his home. Most of the ladies at the dinner party were not to Charlotte's taste and she was not at ease with them. For Thackeray, though, she still had a high regard.

Most people who met her commented on her eyes. Thackeray's daughter called them 'steady'[34] and George Smith, 'kindling'.[35] Anne Thackeray commented how Charlotte could barely reach her father's elbow![36] What would George Richmond, the painter, though, make of her?[37] A beautiful portrait as it turned out, a gift from George Smith to her father.

Richmond captured Charlotte's large hazel-coloured eyes perfectly. It is now the most widely recognised image of Charlotte in the 21st century. Interestingly, Charlotte said that it made her look like Anne.[38] It is often said that a person's soul is caught in their eyes and the soul of the shy, tiny, reticent Charlotte looking away from the artist in the portrait is deeply affecting. This portrait has now become a national treasure and hangs in the National Portrait Gallery in London.

The fact that the great Pre-Raphaelite painter, Sir John Everett Millais, offered to paint Charlotte proves how quickly she had become part of the soul of Great Britain. It was a long journey for the young frightened, lonely, crying girl who had been found at the window at Roe Head to being approached by John Everett Millais for a portrait. It was proof that Charlotte's greatness was, amongst all her critics, being recognised. She turned Millais down and we are left musing on how he would have caught her greatness.[39]

It makes this author ache to think of what the genius who had painted such unforgettable portraits as *Ophelia* (currently valued at at least £30 million), *Christ in the House of his Parents, Bubbles, Caller Herrin', William Ewart Gladstone* and *The Blind Girl* would have created with Charlotte Brontë sitting in front of him! Ah! Choices!

After almost a month Charlotte travelled, after a visit to her friend Ellen at Brookroyd, to Edinburgh. Her publisher, George Smith, had to go to Edinburgh to bring his youngest brother home from school in Scotland for the holidays and he invited Charlotte to join him and his sister. It is obvious that Ellen suspected that there was something of a romance between George and Charlotte by the way Charlotte explains her reasons for going to Scotland! In fact, George's mother became rather alarmed that it might be so.[40] Charlotte denied it and forty-eight years later, in a conversation with Mrs Humphrey Ward, George denied it too: 'No,' he said, 'I never was in the least in love with Charlotte Brontë ... I never was coxcomb enough to suppose that she was in love with me, but I believe that my mother was at one time rather alarmed.'[41] There is some evidence that does point to Charlotte being in love with George Smith despite herself.

Charlotte thoroughly enjoyed her visit to Edinburgh. They followed the Sir Walter Scott trail from his statue on Princes Street to the beautiful rolling hills of the Scottish borders where his home, Abbotsford, is perfectly located by the River Tweed. Did she look up at the exquisite armour of a French Cavalry officer bearing the scars of the battle of Waterloo that was so poignantly hung in the hall? Sir Walter Scott had a deep interest in the Battle of Waterloo and had, like Patrick, visited the battlefield site. Sir Walter Scott's novels had a large influence on Charlotte and her sisters and it must have brought Charlotte deep pleasure to visit his home. Scotland enraptured Charlotte, and she wrote: 'It furnished me with some hours as happy almost as any I ever spent.'

There are millions around the world who would agree with Charlotte's statement that it is the grand Scottish national character that 'gives the land its true charm, its true greatness.'[42] Would that the coming years could have brought Charlotte more of the happiness Scotland had given her.

Twelve
White, Shaking and Voiceless

AUGUST 1850 FOUND Charlotte accepting an invitation to visit the Kay-Shuttleworth's at Brierly Close, the house they had taken in the neighbourhood of Bowness on the shores of Lake Windermere. Again, her father unselfishly urged her to go for he was well aware of the plunge into depression Charlotte's spirit experienced when confined to the parsonage without the company of her sisters and with memories haunting every corner.[1]

It was there at Brierly Close, on the very first evening, that Charlotte was first introduced to another guest, Elizabeth Gaskell. She had sent a copy of *Shirley* to Mrs Gaskell and the author had written a very sympathetic reply when she had finished reading it.

Mrs Gaskell later wrote of the encounter: 'Dark when I got to Windermere station; a drive along the level road to Low-wood; then a stoppage at a pretty house, and then a pretty drawing-room, in which Sir James and Lady Kay-Shuttleworth, and a little lady in a black-silk gown, whom I could not see at first for the dazzle in the room; she came up and shook hands with me at once. I went up to un-bonnet, etc.; came down to tea; the little lady worked away and hardly spoke, but I had time for a good look at her. She is (as she calls herself) *undeveloped,* thin, and more than half a head shorter than I am; soft brown hair, not very dark; eyes (very good and expressive, looking straight and open at you) of the same colour as her hair; a large mouth; the forehead square, broad and rather overhanging. She has a very sweet voice; rather hesitates in choosing her expressions, but when chosen they seem without an effort admirable, and just befitting the occasion; there is nothing overstrained, but perfectly simple.'[2]

Charlotte liked Mrs Gaskell and was glad of her companionship. Sir James took them both out on Lake Windermere. One evening they visited the widow and daughters of the great Christian educator, Dr Thomas Arnold at Fox Howe.[3] Dr Arnold had been the famed headmaster of Rugby School which became in time the model for other English public schools and for boarding schools throughout the Western world. Charlotte travelled by carriage around the Lake District and the holiday did her good and her health improved.

On 19 September, Charlotte wrote her famous *Biographical Notice* for a printing of *Wuthering Heights* and *Agnes Grey* in a single volume. In it she famously identified 'Currer, Ellis and Acton Bell' and sought to defend Emily and Anne from their critics.

At this time Charlotte had been reading the *Life of Thomas Arnold,* sent to her by her publishers. In November she wrote a letter to W S Williams appraising his character. While pointing out his faults, she asked: 'Where can we find justice, firmness, independence, earnestness, sincerity, fuller and purer than in him?' She reckoned 'a hundred such men – fifty – nay, ten or five such righteous men might save any country; might victoriously champion any cause.'[4]

She reckoned Dr Arnold would have been a very useful champion against new moves in the world of Roman Catholicism, as seen in the Pope's appointment of Nicholas Wiseman as Cardinal and Archbishop of Westminster, to which Charlotte was deeply opposed. Such had not been seen since the Reformation and Patrick wrote against it in the *Leeds Intelligencer*, arguing that if the Church of England were overthrown by Dissenters and Catholics all religion would be overthrown and the Goddess of Reason would reign as in the French Revolution.[5]

It would be tempting to stereotype Charlotte as an Anglican bigot but such stereotyping would be a mistake. December 1850 found her back in Ambleside in the Lake District staying with Harriet Martineau, essayist, novelist, journalist, economic and historical writer and atheist. Harriet lived at The Knoll, a house she had designed for herself, and Charlotte stayed for a week.

One evening she found herself dining at the house of Edward Quillinan, son-in-law of William Wordsworth and at the table sat another fascinating guest. His name was Matthew Arnold, son of the famous headmaster of Rugby School.[6] Matthew, a graduate of Oxford University, was no mean poet himself. The following year he was to marry Francis Whiteman and was to become an outstanding Inspector of Schools.

Considered one of the big three Victorian poets along with Tennyson and Robert Browning, he found himself at Dover on his honeymoon night awaiting embarkation for the Continent and listening to the withdrawing tide by his bedroom window. He wrote his famous poem *Dover Beach* on the loss of faith:

The sea is calm tonight.
The tide is full, the moon lies fair
Upon the straits; - on the French coast the light
Gleams and is gone; the cliffs of England stand,
Glimmering and vast, out in the tranquil bay.
Come to the window, sweet is the night air!
Only, from the long line of spray
Where the sea meets the moon-blanch'd land,
Listen! you hear the grating roar
Of pebbles which the waves draw back, and fling,
At their return, up the high strand.
Begin, and cease, and then again begin,
With tremulous cadence slow, and bring
The eternal note of sadness in.

Sophocles long ago
Heard it on the Aegean, and it brought
Into his mind the turbid ebb and flow
Of human misery; we
Find also in the sound a thought,
Hearing it by this distant northern sea.

The Sea of Faith
Was once, too, at the full, and round earth's shore
Lay like the folds of a bright girdle furl'd.

But now I only hear
Its melancholy, long, withdrawing roar,
Retreating, to the breath
Of the night-wind, down the vast edges drear
And naked shingles of the world.

Ah, love let us be true
To one another! for the world, which seems
To lie before us like a land of dreams,
So various, so beautiful, so new,
Hath really neither joy, nor love, nor light,
Nor certitude, nor peace, nor help for pain;
And we are here as on a darkling plain
Swept with confused alarms of struggle and flight,
Where ignorant armies clash by night.[7]

Arnold was, as was Harriet Martineau, part of the ebbing of faith in the nineteenth century when many of the great writers, artists and intellectuals abandoned their belief in Christianity. It all began with the Deism of the Scottish philosopher David Hume and continued with the writings of Charles Darwin and the Higher Criticism of the authenticity of Scripture by German theologians. The litany of gifted people affected included Thomas Carlyle, George Eliot, Thomas Hardy, John Ruskin, George Henry Lewes and many more. Here was a withdrawing belief in the passages of the Gospels containing the miracles of Christ, the prophecies of a Messianic consummation, the virgin birth and the resurrection of the Lord Jesus. The tide of faith withdrew to an ocean of agnosticism and atheism.

In his survey of *Literature and Dogma*, Matthew Arnold begins with a frank acknowledgement that to 're-enthrone the Bible as explained by our current theology, whether learned or popular, is absolutely and forever impossible! – as impossible as to restore the feudal system, or the belief in witches.'[8]

What then of Charlotte, now one of the nation's greatest novelists, daughter of the faithful and evangelical Patrick Brontë, sitting at that table that evening? Did she take the withdrawing tide of the loss of faith that led on to disbelief? Her poem, *Pilate's Wife's Dream*, had imagined what the wife of the Roman Governor in Jerusalem had suffered in a dream because of Christ.[9] Pilate's wife had, of course, pled Christ's innocence. Charlotte wrote:

What is this Hebrew Christ? To me unknown,
His lineage – doctrine – mission – yet how clear,
His Godlike goodness, in his actions shown!
How straight and stainless is his life's career!
The ray of deity that rests on him,
In my eyes makes Olympian glory dim.

The world advances; Greek, or Roman rite
Suffices not the inquiring mind to stay ;
The searching soul demands a purer light
To guide it on its upward, onward way;
Ashamed of sculptured gods – Religion turns
To where the unseen Jehovah's altar burns.

Our faith is rotten, all our rites defiled,
Our temples sullied, and methinks, this man,
With his new ordinance, so wise and mild,
Is come, even as he says, the chaff to fan
And sever from the wheat; but will his faith
Survive the terrors of tomorrow's death?

I feel a firmer trust – a higher hope
Rise in my soul – it dawns with dawning day;
Lo! On the Temple's roof – on Moriah's slope
Appears at length that clear and crimson ray,
Which I so wished for when shut in by night;
Oh, opening skies, I hail, I bless your light!

Part, clouds and shadows! Glorious Sun appear!
Part, mental gloom! Come insight from on high!
Dusk dawn in heaven still strives with daylight clear,
The longing soul, doth still uncertain sigh.
Oh! to behold the truth – that sun divine,
How doth my bosom pant, my spirit pine!

This day, time travails with a mighty birth;
This day, Truth stoops from heaven and visits earth,
Ere night descends, I shall more surely know
What guide to follow, in what path to go;
I wait in hope – I wait in solemn fear,
The oracle of God – the sole – true God – to hear.[9]

What position, then, did Charlotte take in the whole intellectual debate within the nation? How did she react to Harriet Martineau's reading of the proofs of her new book (co-authored with Henry Atkinson, *Letters on the Law of Man's Social Nature and Development*) at her home later that very evening?

In a letter to James Taylor written on 11 February 1851, Charlotte is unequivocal: 'Of the impression this book has made on me, I will not now say much. It is the first exposition of avowed atheism and materialism I have ever read; the first unequivocal declaration of disbelief in the existence of a God or a Future Life I have ever seen. In judging of such exposition and declaration, one would wish entirely to put aside the sort of instinctive horror they awaken, and to consider them in an impartial spirit and collected mood. This I find it difficult to do. The strangest thing is that we are called on to rejoice over this hopeless blank – to receive this bitter bereavement as great gain – to welcome this unutterable desolation as a state of pleasant freedom. Who *could* do this if he would? Who *would* do it if he could?'[10]

What then, incidentally, of Edward Quillinan the host of that microcosmic evening of 19th century intellectual life in England? We can certainly speak for his wife Dora who had died but three years previously on 9 July 1847. She had been hugely influenced by the poetry of Charlotte Elliott who, on hearing of her illness, had sent her a copy of her poem, *Just As I Am*, which was to become one of the best known evangelical hymns in history. Written when Miss Elliott was experiencing doubt, the poem highlights the certainties brought by faith in Christ alone:

Just as I am, without one plea,
But that Thy blood was shed for me,
And that Thou bidd'st me come to Thee,
O Lamb of God, I come! I come!

Just as I am, and waiting not
To rid my soul of one dark blot,
To Thee, whose blood can cleanse each spot,
O Lamb of God, I come! I come!

Just as I am, though tossed about,
With many a conflict, many a doubt,
Fightings within, and fears without,
O Lamb of God, I come! I come!

Just as I am, poor, wretched, blind;
Sight, riches, healing of the mind,
Yea, all I need, in Thee to find,
O Lamb of God, I come! I come!

Just as I am, Thou wilt receive,
Wilt welcome, pardon, cleanse, relieve:
Because Thy promise I believe,
O Lamb of God, I come! I come!

Just as I am, Thy love unknown
Hath broken every barrier down;
Now, to be Thine, yea, Thine alone,
O Lamb of God, I come! I come!

Dora's father, William Wordsworth, the Poet Laureate, did not at first like the poem but he later said that his daughter had died with great peace because of it. In fact, while she lived she talked continuously about the poem to people all around her in Grasmere and the poem became known as Dora's Hymn. Her tombstone in St Oswald's church cemetery in Grasmere carries to this day the symbolism of the poem that meant so much to her; there is a cross and beneath the cross a lamb, symbolising the death of Christ on our behalf. Beneath the cross and the lamb are the words of Christ's beautiful invitation from John 6:37, 'Him that cometh to me I will in no wise cast out.' It all catches perfectly the spirit of Miss Elliott's poem that carries at the end of each stanza the line: 'O Lamb of God, I come! I come!'[11]

There was certainly more to that evening spent at Edward Quillinan's home in September 1850 than met the eye. One thing is certain: the long, melancholic retreating tide of the loss of faith had not swept Charlotte Brontë out with it as the mid-century Christmas season approached.

The New Year brought the red-haired clerk of Smith, Elder & Co. back to Haworth, not to collect a new manuscript from Charlotte but to propose to her. This was a third proposal of marriage but Charlotte's veins did not run fire, rather they ran ice. 'Could I ever feel enough for James Taylor,' she wrote to Ellen, 'to accept him as a husband? Friendship – gratitude – esteem – I have; but each moment he came near me, and that I could see his eyes fastened on me, my veins ran ice. Now that he is away, I feel far more gently towards him; it is only close by that I grow rigid, stiffening with a strange mixture of apprehension and anger, which nothing softens but his retreat, and a perfect subduing of his manner. I did not want to be proud, nor intend to be proud, but I was forced to be so. More true it is, that we are overruled by One above us; and that in his hands our very will is as clay in the hands of the potter.'[12]

Patrick now in his seventy-fifth year and still preaching twice on a Sunday continued to campaign for pure water for Haworth, a campaign that was frustrated by wealthy people seeking exemption from the water-rates which would have to be paid as a result.[13] In May, Charlotte returned once more to London. She went to a lecture by Thackeray where she was rather too audibly introduced to his mother as 'Jane Eyre.' Charlotte was deeply embarrassed as every eye turned upon her. Charlotte berated Thackeray for his behaviour the next day.

She visited the Great Exhibition at the specially constructed Crystal Palace in Hyde Park which had even enclosed full-grown trees. In fact, she visited the Exhibition five times during her month-long stay in London. It was opened by Queen Victoria on 1 May and closed on 15 October 1851. Organised by Prince Albert, Henry Cole, Francis Fuller, Charles Dilke and other members of the Royal Society for the Encouragement of Arts, Manufacturers and Commerce as a celebration of modern industrial technology and design, the Exhibition was visited by six million people. It has since become the symbol of the Victorian Age.

The 'Great Exhibition of Works of Industry in all Nations' did not deeply impress Charlotte. She wrote: 'I went there five times and certainly saw some interesting things and the 'coup d'oeil' is striking and bewildering enough; but I never was able to get up any raptures on the subject, and each renewed visit was made under coercion rather than my own free will. It is an excessively bustling place; and, after all, its wonders appeal too exclusively to the eye, and rarely touch the heart or head. I make an exception to the last assertion, in favour of those who possess a large range of scientific knowledge. Once I went with Sir David Brewster, and perceived that he looked on objects with other eyes than mine.'[15]

One Sunday afternoon found Charlotte listening to the great Swiss evangelical preacher, Jean-Henri D'Aubigné, a famed historian of the Reformation. D'Aubigné, once a pastor in Brussels and a preacher to the Court, was now a Professor of Church History in Geneva and frequently visited England. A lot lay behind Charlotte's summary of hearing him preach in French: 'I went to hear D'Aubigné the great Protestant French preacher; it was pleasant – half sweet, half sad – and strangely suggestive to hear the French language once more.'[16]

Charlotte also went to a lecture by Cardinal Wiseman and recalled the experience with derisory scorn.[17]   Charlotte was asked to breakfast with Samuel Rogers who, the previous year at eighty-four-years-of-age, had been offered the position of Poet Laureate on Wordsworth's death. He declined the appointment due to his age. The daughter of the man from Drumballyroney in Ireland was now at the heart of the literary establishment as she dined with the friend of Byron, Wordsworth, Scott, Talleyrand, Edward Burke, Henry Grattan and her hero, the Duke of Wellington.

Charlotte did not succumb to being patronised by the society hostesses in London and eschewed any obligation to them. She eventually left London on 2 June and went to stay for two days with Mrs Gaskell in Manchester.[18]   Her relationship with this formidable writer was to eventually play a very important role in how the world was to view her.

Poor Charlotte never found it easy to settle back into Haworth life after her exposure to London society. Who could blame her?   Her friend Ellen came to stay and, later in September, Miss Margaret Wooler. Charlotte again made an attempt to continue writing her novel *Villette* which had been in the writing since 1849. It was again abandoned. In a letter to Mrs Gaskell that September, she wrote: 'You charge me to write about myself. What can I say on that precious topic? My health is pretty good. My spirits are not always alike. Nothing happens to me. I hope and expect little in this world, and am thankful that I do not despond and suffer more.'[19]

By November, Charlotte was ill with inflammation of her liver and through pills given to her by her doctor, she suffered mercury poisoning.[20] She had a holiday at Brookroyd with Ellen which helped and, despite all her setbacks, she completed her draft of the first volume of *Villette* by 29 March 1852.[21] She went to Filey once more for a holiday and visited Anne's grave at Scarborough, just before the anniversary of her death. She found five errors in the inscription on the tombstone and ordered the stone to be refaced and relettered. Charlotte was still suffering ill health and walked on the sands of Filey trying not to feel too desolate and melancholy. It wasn't easy for that is how she really felt.[22]

It was now back to work on her novel *Villette* when her father had a minor stroke. Charlotte nursed him back to health and wrote on. It was lonely hard work again, plagued with depression. She sent the second volume of the novel to her publishers on 26 October 1852. She tried to have the book published anonymously, but lost the battle.[23]

It did not take George Smith long to see himself in the character of Graham Bretton and his mother as Mrs Bretton. The heroine, Lucy Snowe, of course, almost falls in love with Graham Bretton in the novel. George Smith was, fortunately, not annoyed with Charlotte using her visits to his home as fodder for her novel.[24] Encouraged, Charlotte ploughed on with the third volume and sent it to him on 20 November.[25] Though he was disappointed with the plot of the third volume, George Smith did not ask for a rewrite.[26] A relieved Charlotte now relaxed and looked forward to a visit to London after Christmas. Then came a bombshell.

Twelve days before Christmas 1852, Charlotte was sitting after tea in her own sitting room at the Haworth parsonage when there was a tap on the door. There stood the Rev A B Nicholls. 'Like lightning,' Charlotte told Mrs Gaskell, 'it flashed upon me what was coming. He entered. He stood before me. What his words were you can imagine; his manner you can hardly realise, nor can I forget it. He made me, for the first time, feel what it costs a man to declare affection when he doubts response ... the spectacle of one, ordinarily so statue-like, thus trembling, stirred, and overcome, gave me a strange shock. I could only entreat him to leave me then, and promise a reply on the morrow. I asked him if he had spoken to Papa. He said he dared not. I think I half led, half put him out of the room.'[27]

Charlotte went immediately to her father and told him of his curate's proposal. If ever veins were running fire in Brontë blood, this was the night. Charlotte described the ensuing conversation: 'Agitation and anger disproportionate to the occasion ensued – if I had loved Mr N and heard such epithets applied to him as were used, it would have transported me past my patience – as it was – my blood boiled with a sense of injustice – but Papa worked himself into a state not to be trifled with; the veins on his temples started up like whip-cord and his eyes became suddenly bloodshot. I made haste to promise that Mr Nicholls should on the morrow have a distinct refusal.'[28] He did.

Why was Patrick so angry? To start with, the curate had not asked him for his daughter's hand. Here was a cocktail of jealousy and snobbery on Patrick's part that was lethal. Poor Mr Nicholls was now, to the consternation of his landlady, actually refusing to eat because he was so lovesick. Patrick sent him a cruel note, but Charlotte balanced it by slipping in one of her own telling him that while he must never expect her to reciprocate his feelings, she 'wished to disdain participation in sentiments calculated to give him pain.' She also exhorted him 'to maintain his courage and spirits.'[29]

It can't have been easy for the poor man. Charlotte defended him and the village people were torn between two opposing parties. Martha Brown was bitter against the curate, John Brown said he would like to shoot him. Mr Nicholls offered his resignation to Patrick and then offered to take it back again.

Yes, Patrick replied, he could have it back on one condition: that he gave his written promise to never broach the subject of marrying Charlotte either to him or her again! Mr Nicholl's love for Charlotte was too deep for that. He refused.[30] It must have been quite a Christmas at Haworth. We smile at the situation now but it was no laughing matter for Charlotte, caught between an implacable father and his passionate curate. She accepted with relief an invitation from Mrs Smith to visit London again, and fled!

On this visit, her last, Charlotte decided as she was to put it, to see 'the *real*' rather than the '*decorative*' side of life. She visited Newgate and Pentonville prisons and two hospitals, the Foundling and Bethlehem. She also requested to see the Bank of England, the Exchange and Rothschild's. While in London, Charlotte corrected the proofs of her novel *Villette* and magnanimously persuaded her publisher to hold back its publication until after the publication of Mrs Gaskell's novel, *Ruth*, to avoid a clash of clash of unfair comparisons in reviews across the country.[31] *Villette* was eventually published on 28 January 1853 and, perhaps, Mrs Gaskell's comment best sums up its content. '*Villette*,' she wrote, 'which, if less interesting as a mere story than *Jane Eyre*, displays yet more of the extraordinary genius of the author.'[32]

Charlotte must have made the return journey to Haworth with deepest trepidation. She arranged for her friend Ellen to meet her at Keighley station and Ellen went home with her to stay for two weeks. Two are indeed better than one.[33] Not only did Charlotte have to face a deeply disgruntled father but she had to face the coming reviews of her book. Mostly they were favourable, though Harriet Martineau's review in the *Daily News* really stunned Charlotte. She 'writhed under what she felt to be injustice.'[34] Harriet accused Charlotte of dominating all the female characters in *Villette* with 'the need of being loved.' She argued that women of all ages in real life have other 'substantial, heartfelt interests.'[35] Charlotte defended her position with vehemence. The quarrel, sadly, led to an end of their friendship.

A visit of the Bishop of Ripon, Dr Charles Longley, to Haworth where he stayed overnight with the Brontës brought quite a lot of local clergy to the parsonage, including the Rev Nicholls. There were flashes of temper several times when he spoke to Patrick and later, in a letter to Ellen, Charlotte berated him for demeaning himself 'not quite pleasantly.' She criticised him for making no effort 'to struggle with his dejection.' 'If Mr N. be a good man at bottom – it is a sad thing that Nature has not given him the faculty to put goodness into a more attractive form.'[36]

The lovesick curate had applied to the Society for the Propagation of the Gospel to be a missionary in Australia and, to be fair to Patrick, he had written him an excellent, if not entirely effusive, reference. Mr Nicholls withdrew his obligation in April 1852 hoping in his heart that Charlotte would change her mind. He now declared that he would seek a curacy elsewhere.[37] Would Charlotte change her mind? In the same month she wrote to Ellen saying that she pitied Mr Nicholls 'inexpressibly.' Pity, though, is very often akin to love. Charlotte told Ellen she was 'entirely passive' in the circumstance and argued that her conscience would not allow her to take one step in opposition to her father's will – 'blended as that will is with the most bitter and unreasonable prejudices.' 'So,' she wrote, 'I just leave the matter where we must leave all important matters.'[39] Pity and prayer were to lead to quite a story.

Charlotte went off to Manchester to stay with the Gaskell's for a week and came home the better for it. Her friendship with

Mrs Gaskell had deepened and blossomed. When she returned to Haworth, the Rev Nicholls was in his last month in the curacy and on Whit Sunday Charlotte went to church to take communion. The Rev Nicholls was leading the service.

Charlotte wrote: 'I got a lesson not to be repeated. He struggled, faltered, then lost command over himself – stood before my eyes and in the sight of all the communicants white, shaking, voiceless – Papa was not there, thank God! Joseph Redman spoke some words to him, he made a great effort, but could only with difficulty whisper and falter through the service. I suppose he thought this would be the last time; he goes either this week or the next. I heard the women sobbing round and I could not quite check my own tears.

'What had happened was reported to Papa either by Joseph Redman or John Brown – it excited only anger – and such expressions as "unmanly driveller." Compassion or relenting is no more to be looked for than sap from firewood.'[40]

At a following Whitsuntide social occasion at the church, Patrick spoke civilly to Mr Nicholls but he cut him short. 'I am afraid,' wrote Charlotte, 'both are unchristian in their mutual feelings.'[41] She was right.

Mr Nicholls was presented with a gold watch before his departure at a special ceremony in the National Schoolroom.[42] He called at the parsonage the next evening to hand over the deeds of the National School and to say farewell. Again Charlotte gave Ellen the detail. In the circumstances Charlotte decided not to enter the parlour while Mr Nicholls talked with her father and he left without seeing her. 'But, perceiving that he stayed long before going out at the gate, and remembering his long grief, I took courage and went out, trembling and miserable. I found him leaning against the garden door in a paroxysm of anguish, sobbing as women never sob. Of course, I went straight to him. Very few words were interchanged, those few barely articulate. Several things I would have liked to ask him were swept entirely from my memory. Poor fellow! But he wanted such hope and such encouragement as I could not give him. Still, I trust he must know now that I am not cruelly blind and indifferent to his constancy and grief ... however he is gone – gone, and there's an end of it.'[43]

Mr Nicholls, in fact, left Haworth the next morning at 6 o'clock.

Thirteen
The Seduced and The Blind

THE EVENTS that now followed would not have been out of place in any Brontë novel. Charlotte turned to writing once more, attempting a new story entitled *Willie Ellin*.[1] Charlotte's health showed signs of stress and she had to take to her bed for ten days with influenza.[2] Stress also showed its presence in Patrick's life because he suffered a second stroke which immediately blinded him. His sight never fully recovered again.[3]

Charlotte was now feeling isolated and depressed and when called 'an alien, it might seem, from society and amenable to none of its laws' by a review in the *Christian Remembrancer*,[4] she lashed back in a defensive letter, highlighting the fact that the devastation of death in her family and the present state of health of her father had occasioned her narrow domestic circumstance.[5]

By July, it seems, Charlotte had abandoned her new story. She had also given in to let Mr Nicholls clandestinely correspond with her.[6] This erupted into a quarrel with a jealous Ellen Nussey who was deeply opposed to Charlotte showing an interest in him. Soon Charlotte and Ellen stopped visiting each other and also, sadly, stopped writing to each other as the quarrel rose in temperature.[7] The summer of 1853 found Charlotte on holiday with Miss Wooler at Ilkley after a much disrupted attempt to holiday in Scotland and York with the Joe Taylor family.[8]

A much welcomed four-day visit from Mrs Gaskell to the parsonage in September brought much needed company to Charlotte. Unfortunately, it also brought the world, as already noted, an often false portrait of Patrick when Mrs Gaskell eventually wrote her much acclaimed *Life of Charlotte Brontë*. It has been pointed out that she came close to Patrick and Charlotte when their relationship was at its lowest ebb and this coloured her perception of the five-decade serving Christian minister.[9] She had also, of course, listened to false stories about him from a disgruntled servant Patrick had dismissed and from Lady Kay-Shuttleworth.

In November, Charlotte was absolutely shattered to learn that her publisher George Smith was to be married to the beautiful Elizabeth Blakeway, daughter of a wealthy London wine merchant. Charlotte had suspected that something was up and had written to his mother to find out what ailed him after she had received a letter from him.[10] Charlotte, on the verge of a trip to London, cancelled it of her own volition. Her letter to him on 10 December 1853 says it all: 'My dear Sir, In great happiness, as in great grief - words of sympathy should be few. Accept my meed of congratulation – and believe me. Sincerely yours, C Brontë.'[11]

Her family decimated, Ellen gone out of her life, her confidant George Smith to be married, Charlotte now turned to face the one great blazing question in her life: in her isolation and loneliness, how would she deal with the unrequited love of Mr Nicholls?

Her first move was to inform her father that she had been writing to the curate for the last six months. After a few days, Patrick, amazingly, gave Charlotte leave to continue writing to Mr Nicholls.[12] Eventually, and very reluctantly, he agreed to a meeting between them. In June 1854, Mr Nicholls stayed for ten days with his friend, the Rev Grant, at the nearby Oxenhope vicarage. In the face of rising esteem and growing affection for Mr Nicholls, Patrick had to relent and allow Mr Nicholls to visit the parsonage at Haworth.[13]

Amid deep snows[14] Mr Nicholls courted Charlotte's heart and he returned to the curacy he had taken up at Kirk Smeaton in Yorkshire encouraged but well aware that he had not yet conquered.

Mercifully, Charlotte now began to communicate with her old friend Ellen Nussey once more.[15] Two weeks before Easter 1854, Mr Nicholls arrived once more at Oxenhope. This time he came, he saw, and he conquered. Charlotte said 'yes' but insisted that Mr Nicholls return to Haworth as Patrick's curate. Charlotte also insisted that Patrick would continue to live at the parsonage after her marriage. Her veins must have run a lot of fire as she verbalised her wishes but she achieved them as she desired. One thing is certain, Mr Nicholls must have truly loved Charlotte Brontë to endure what he endured.[16]

One can only conclude that Charlotte was not in love with Mr Nicholls when she married him; rather, she hoped to love him. This conclusion comes because of the following letter to Ellen: 'I am still very calm, very inexpectant. What I taste of happiness is of the soberest order. I trust to love my husband, I am grateful for his tender love to me, I believe him to be an affectionate, a conscientious, a high-principled man and, if with all this, I should yield to regrets – that fine talents, congenial views, tastes and thoughts are not added – it seems to me I should be most presumptuous and thankless. Providence offers me this destiny. Doubtless, then, it is the best for me ...'[17]

Here one catches an air of Charlotte marrying for affection rather than love, of marrying for companionship rather than from a great passion. She described her happiness as 'of the soberest order'; this was no Jane Eyre wanting to marry Rochester. There is a sadness in it, even though the marriage was to lead to a great deal of happiness. That sadness is best summed up in her words to Mrs Gaskell, a few months before: 'We talked about the different courses through which life ran. She said, in her own composed manner, as if she had accepted the theory as a fact, that she believed some were appointed beforehand to sorrow and much disappointment; that it did not fall to the lot of all – as Scripture told us – to have their lines fall in pleasant places; that it was well for those who had rougher paths, to perceive that such was God's will concerning them, and try to moderate their expectations, leaving hope to those of a different doom, and seeking patience and resignation as the virtues they were to cultivate.

'I took a different view: I thought that human lots were more equal than she imagined; that to some happiness and sorrow came in strong patches of light and shadow (so to speak), while in the lives of others they were pretty equally blended throughout. She smiled, and shook her head, and said she was trying to school herself against ever anticipating any pleasure; that it was better to be brave and submit faithfully; there was some good reason, which we should know in time, why sorrow and disappointment were to be the lot of some on earth. It was better to acknowledge this, and face out the truth in a religious faith.'[18]

One also concludes that George Smith was the man who had Charlotte's heart and her cold business-like letters to him at this time more than hint at a sense of betrayal. In *Villette*, Lucy Snowe loved Dr John but married the 'crabbed Professor.' Was not Charlotte's former letter to George Smith when he enquired of the fate of Dr John (based, as he very well knew, on himself) not prophetic? She wrote: 'Lucy must not marry Dr John; he is far too youthful, handsome, bright-spirited and sweet-tempered; he is a "curled darling" of Nature and of Fortune; he must draw a prize in life's lottery; his wife must be young, rich and pretty; he must be made very happy indeed. If Lucy marries anybody – it must be the Professor – a man in whom there is much to forgive – much to "put up with."'[19]

The wedding date was set for Thursday 29 June 1854, a few days after Patrick's interim curate, the Rev de Renzy's departure from Haworth. We now have an interesting source to draw from regarding the wedding day. In his eighty-sixth year a Haworth resident called John Robinson gave an interview to the *Keighley News*. The interview was published on 27 October 1923.

He told the intriguing story of how as a young person he had been given private lessons by Mr Nicholls. On the morning of Charlotte and Arthur Nicholl's wedding he was way-led in Church Lane in Haworth by John Brown, Branwell's old drinking partner, and told of the coming wedding ceremony that was set for 8.00am that morning. He was told to go to the top of the hill and look for three men approaching the church, namely, the Rev Nicholls, the Rev Grant and the Rev Sutcliffe Snowden. When they appeared he was to run to the parsonage and let the bride and her party know that all was now ready. Then he was to go and fetch the Parish Clerk, Joseph Redman, and bring him to the church.[20]

It is hard to credit but Patrick decided *the night before* that he would not go to the wedding ceremony and Charlotte accepted his excuse of ill health.[21] Perhaps the truth was that he couldn't face going to the wedding ceremony. Miss Wooller gave Charlotte away in his place, and Ellen Nussey, who had opposed the marriage, was bridesmaid. The Rev Sutcliffe Snowden, vicar of Hebden Bridge, conducted the wedding ceremony.

What were Charlotte's thoughts as her 8.00am wedding ceremony got under way? 'I require and charge you both (as ye will answer at the dreadful Day of Judgment, when the secrets of all hearts shall be disclosed), that if either of you know any impediment why ye may not lawfully be joined in matrimony,' said the Rev Snowden, 'ye do now confess it; for be ye well assured that so many as are coupled together otherwise than God's Word doth allow, are not joined together by God, neither is their matrimony lawful.'[22]

Did not Charlotte's mind switch to the most memorable wedding ceremony ever written in fiction where, at this point, Jane Eyre lost Rochester? It would be hard to believe it didn't. No voice rose to object but, somehow, one imagines the silent voice of Patrick yards away in his parsonage 'thundering.' It added a sickening twist to the story of Charlotte Brontë. She deserved better treatment from a man who all his life had been a consistently loving father and a conscientiously faithful minister of the Christian church. One feels that he failed her just when she needed him most. We all have our dark sides and this, one feels, was Patrick's.

Did the same passion run in Charlotte's veins as that which ran in Jane's as she passed Rochester's bedroom on the night that followed the horror of the disrupted wedding ceremony?

'I would have got past Mr Rochester's chamber without a pause; but my heart momentarily stopping its beat at that threshold, my foot was forced to stop also. No sleep was there: the inmate was walking restlessly from wall to wall; and again and again he sighed while I listened. There was a heaven – a temporary heaven – in this room for me, if I chose: I had but to go in and to say, "Mr Rochester, I will love you and live with you through life till death," and a fount of rapture would spring to my lips. I thought of this.'[23]

It raises the interesting and constant question: Is a marriage based on companionship better than one based on romance and passion?

The news of the wedding 'had slipped abroad before the little party came out of the church,' writes Mrs Gaskell, 'and many old and humble friends were there, seeing her look "like a snowdrop" as they say. Her dress was white embroidered muslin, with a lace mantle, and white bonnet trimmed with green leaves, which perhaps might suggest the resemblance to the pale wintry flower.'[24]

A wedding breakfast followed, with flowers scattered by Ellen and bouquets decorating the parsonage arranged by Martha. A carriage and pair arrived to take Mr and Mrs Arthur Nicholls to Keighley station and their honeymoon. Charlotte, we learn, in her going-away outfit wore a dress made from silver-grey silk with a lavender tinge to it, with large sleeves narrowing to the cuff, a full skirt, tight waist and velvet trimmed neck.[25] She was on her way with the man she hoped she would love. How would it all end? Sooner than either could have imagined.

The couple, after exploring the North Wales Coast and the valleys of Snowdonia,[35] sailed from Anglesey on the packet steamer for Dublin. Mr Nicholls took his bride to see Trinity College where he had been a student and his brother, manager of the Grand Canal in Dublin, joined them on their visit to their home town of Banagher. Two cousins also joined them on the journey, including one, whom Charlotte said, was 'a pretty lady-like girl with gentle English manners.'[26]

The Anglo-Irish world to which Mr Nicholls introduced Charlotte greatly surprised her. The large house in which her husband had been raised by his uncle impressed her. 'I must say I like my new relations. My dear husband, too, appears in a new light in his own country. More than once I have had a deep pleasure in hearing his praises on all sides. Some of the old servants and followers of the family tell me I am a most fortunate person; for that I have got one of the best gentlemen in the country ... I trust I feel thankful to God for having enabled me to make what seems a right choice, and I pray to be enabled to repay as I ought the affectionate devotion of a truthful, honourable man.'[27]   The word 'seems', though, carries the element of sadness. She had not expected this much happiness or realised the social status held by her husband's family.

Anthony Trollope, the great English novelist of *The Barchester Chronicles* fame, once lived in Banagher but his eye was no keener in observation than that of the newly-married rector's daughter from Haworth. The Rev and Mrs Nicholls moved on to visit Limerick and Kilkee, one of the most famous seaside resorts in Ireland. Charlotte relished the mile-long horseshoe bay protected from the Atlantic coast weather by the Duggerna Reef, one of the safest bathing spots in Europe.[28] Staying at the West End Hotel, Charlotte walked on the cliffs and sat rug-wrapped viewing the ocean below with its magnificent breakers. Her letters reveal the deep and growing relationship with her husband that has obviously become full of humour and considerate kindness.[29]

They again moved on across the southwest corner of Ireland visiting Tarbert, Tralee, Killarney, Glengarriff and Cork.

Charlotte loved the scenery, even finding parts of it better than she had imagined.[30] Her idyll nearly ended, though, in the Gap of Dunloe. Arthur had to warn Charlotte not to go too near the edge of a cliff at Kilkee for she was, it seems, daring. Now her guide warned her to dismount from her horse as the path at Dunloe was very steep. She did not feel afraid and declined to dismount. 'My horse seemed to go mad,' she wrote later. As the horse panicked, Arthur concentrated on trying to calm it. The horse would have none of it and poor Charlotte found herself thrown to the ground. Arthur, on realising what was happening, had the presence of mind to let the horse go and it leapt over Charlotte and she escaped unhurt but was deeply shocked. That independent streak in Charlotte had led to her being nearly trampled to death.[31]

It must have been heartening for the couple, on returning to Haworth, to find so many people calling to wish them well. Charlotte told Ellen: 'Both Mr Nicholls and myself wished much to make some response for the hearty welcome and general goodwill shown by the parishioners on his return; accordingly, the Sunday and day scholars and teachers, the church-ringers, singers etc., to the number of five hundred, were asked to tea and supper in the schoolroom. They seemed to enjoy it much, and it was very pleasant to see their happiness. One of the villagers, in proposing my husband's health, described him as a *"consistent Christian and a kind gentleman."* I own the words touched me deeply, and I thought (as I know *you* would have thought had you been present) that to merit and win such a character was better than to earn either wealth, or fame, or power. I am disposed to echo that high but simple eulogium ...

'My dear father was not yet well when we returned from Ireland. I am, however, most thankful to say that he is better now. May God preserve him to us yet for some years! The wish for his continued life, together with a certain solicitude for his happiness and health, seems, I scarcely know why, even stronger in me now than before I was married. Papa has taken no duty since we returned; and each time I see Mr Nicholls put on gown or surplice, I feel comforted to think that this marriage has secured papa good aid in his old age.'[32]

It is moving to read that Charlotte had now pulled away from the virtually intolerable loneliness of recent years. Now that she was preoccupied with her husband's life and duties, helping him in every way she could, she was drawn away from herself. The tug of what wealth or fame or power promised had receded in the rising happiness she was experiencing in her marriage.[33]

Ellen came to stay for two weeks but, unfortunately, Mr Nicholls now ruled that she must burn all of Charlotte's letters to her or he would censor them.[34] She promised only if he would pledge no censorship. Mr Nicholls agreed, but Ellen, it seems, convinced herself that he continued to censor and therefore she did not feel obliged to burn the letters.[35] This only fuelled Ellen's animosity towards him, something that was to continue throughout the rest of her life.

December 1854 found Patrick, Mr Nicholls and Charlotte busy in helping to raise voluntary subscriptions for the benefit of the wounded, widows and orphans of the Crimean War.[36] Illness had invaded the homes of Ellen and the Taylors, with Joe facing death and Ellen's sister, Mercy, gravely ill with typhus.[37] For a change, all was well at the Haworth parsonage with Charlotte writing to Ellen on Boxing Day: 'Arthur joins me in sincere good wishes for a happy Christmas and many of them to you and yours. He is well, thank God, and so am I – and he is "my dear boy" certainly – dearer now than he was six months ago; in three days we shall actually have been married that length of time!'[38]

Back in November Charlotte had taken a walk with Arthur to see the melted snow pouring over the waterfall at Sladen Beck.

The rain began to fall when they got to the waterfall and continued as they walked the three miles home. Though she changed her clothes immediately she reached the parsonage, Charlotte caught a chill which passed.[39]

In January, Charlotte now began to experience sensations of perpetual nausea and ever-recurring faintness.[40] A doctor was called and confirmed what normally would have been the best news Charlotte could have heard, she was pregnant. Yet, as was constantly the case in the Brontë family, rising happiness was crushed by incredible sorrow. Charlotte now experienced increasing sickness and her health began to seriously deteriorate. Her husband sent for the notable Bradford physician, Dr MacTurk, who pronounced that her illness 'would be of some duration' but that there was no immediate danger.[41]

'About the third week in March,' wrote Mrs Gaskell, 'there was a change; a low wandering delirium came on, and in it she begged constantly for food and even for stimulants. She swallowed eagerly now; but it was too late. Wakening for an instant from this stupor of intelligence, she saw her husband's woe-worn face, and caught the sound of some murmured words of prayer that God would spare her. "Oh!" she whispered forth, "I am not going to die, am I? He will not separate us, we have been so happy."'

Early on Saturday morning, 31 March 1855, the solemn tolling of Haworth church-bell spoke forth the fact of her death to the villagers who had known her from a child, and whose hearts shivered within them as they thought of the two sitting desolate and alone in the old grey house.[42] Charlotte Brontë died just three weeks short of her thirty-ninth birthday. She had been married for just eighteen months.[43]

Charlotte was buried on Wednesday 4 April amidst a thronged church and churchyard. 'Her whom, not many months ago, they had looked at as a pale white bride, entering on a new life with trembling happy hope.'[44] Her burial service was taken by her friend, the Rev Sutcliffe Snowden.[45] Afterwards, a funeral sermon was preached by the headmaster of Skipton Grammar School, the Rev William Cartman, on the text, 'And all wept and bewailed her' from Luke 8:52.[46]

While Charlotte had endured almost indescribable suffering during her lifetime, the congregation at her funeral service was deeply representative of what her life had meant to people. Two girls in that crowded throng epitomised the true heart of this great writer. Mrs Gaskell, to her eternal credit, highlighted both of them. Amidst all the millions of words written about Charlotte, these words portray perfectly the compassionate kindness that often flowed in her veins:

'Among those humble friends who passionately grieved over the dead, was a village girl who had been seduced some little time before, but who had found a holy sister in Charlotte. She had sheltered her with her help, her counsel, her strengthening words, had ministered to her needs in her time of trial. Bitter, bitter was the grief of this poor young woman, when she heard that her friend was sick unto death, and deep is her mourning until this day. A blind girl, living some four miles from Haworth, loved Mrs Nicholls so dearly that, with many cries and entreaties, she implored those about her to lead her along the roads, and over the moor-paths, that she might hear the last solemn words, "Earth to earth, ashes to ashes, dust to dust; in sure and certain hope of the resurrection of eternal life, through our Lord Jesus Christ." '[47]

If only those two girls had been helped by Charlotte, was not her life worth living?

FOURTEEN

Perhaps

MRS GASKELL'S *Life of Charlotte Brontë* was published on 25 March 1857 and caused a sensation. In a sense it still does for, despite some inaccuracies about Patrick, later rectified, it gets incredibly close to Charlotte. Patrick was amazingly magnanimous about it all. Of the rectified third edition, he said it was 'every way worthy of what one Great Woman, should have written of Another, and that it ought to stand, and will stand in the first rank of biographies, to the end of time.'[1]

Charlotte's novel, *The Professor*, was at last published in June 1857, Mr Nicholl's having conscientiously edited the text.[2] It did not rate highly with the critics but remains a benchmark against which the progress of Charlotte's writing gift had flourished by the time she wrote *Villette.*

Lots of controversy arose around Mrs Gaskell's biography even throughout the rest of Patrick's lifetime: Lady Scott threatened to sue,[3] Carus Wilson's son challenged the portrayal of life at Cowan Bridge in the press,[4] William Dearden (a friend of Patrick's) ferociously attacked Mrs Gaskell's portrayal of his friend through the press,[5] Harriet Martineau wasn't dormant either amidst all the controversy, complaining in print that Charlotte's statements about her, quoted in the book, were not true.[6]

Patrick and Arthur Nicholls, though, survived it all, amazingly becoming extremely close friends. They both became famous in the light of the biography and many visitors began to arrive in Haworth seeking what was now fast becoming the Brontë legend, not least the Americans who still seek it.

Patrick preached his last sermon in Haworth Parish Church on 30 October 1859 in his eighty-second year. His bronchial condition now made it impossible for him to continue.[7] It was an incredible achievement showing great faith and unswerving commitment to his Christian calling. He survived the winter of 1859 but, by the following August, was virtually confined to bed.[8] Amazingly resilient, he also survived the severe winter of 1860 and reached his eighty-fourth birthday on St Patrick's Day, 17 March 1861, amidst heavy snow which reached the tops of the walls in Haworth.[9] The snows on the slopes of Death were also approaching. On 29 June 1861 the Victorian age's favourite poetess, Elizabeth Barrett Browning, died in the arms of her husband Robert in Florence in Italy.

That autumn, Browning wrote his majestic poem, *Prospice*, as he reflected on the death of his wife. It awesomely presents Browning's Christian faith in the face of life's greatest enemy and, one feels, perfectly encapsulates Patrick Brontë's attitude to death. In fact, few Christian ministers can ever have conducted so many funeral services during their lifetime.

Throughout all of these funeral services, Patrick would have read the words of Job from the Book of Common Prayer: 'For I know that my redeemer liveth, and that he shall stand at the latter day upon the earth; and though after my skin worms destroy this body, yet in the flesh shall I see God: whom I shall see for myself, and mine eyes shall behold, and not another.'[10] The *Book of Common Prayer* also asks: 'And now, Lord, what is my hope?' It answers in the words of Psalm 39:7, 'Truly, my hope is even in Thee.'

Now Patrick faced death himself and Browning's words are apposite:

Fear death? to feel the fog in my throat,
The mist in my face,
When the snows begin, and the blasts denote
I am nearing the place,
The power of the night, the press of the storm,
The post of the foe;
Where he stands, the Arch Fear in a visible form;
Yet the strong man must go:
For the journey is done and the summit attained,
And the barriers fall,
Though a battle's to fight ere the guerdon be gained,
The reward of it all.
I was ever a fighter, so – one fight more,
The best and the last!
I would hate that death bandaged my eyes, and forbore,
And bade me creep past.
No! let me taste the whole of it, fare like my peers,
The heroes of old,

Bear the brunt, in a minute pay glad life's arrears
Of pain, darkness and cold.
For sudden the worst turns the best to the brave,
The black minute's at end,
And the elements' rage, the fiend-voices that rave,
Shall dwindle, shall blend,
Shall change, shall become first a peace out of pain.
Then a light, then thy breast,
O thou soul of my soul! I shall clasp thee again,
And with God be the rest![11]

On Friday 7 June 1861, Patrick was seized with convulsions and slipped into a state of unconsciousness. He died between 2.00 and 3.00 that afternoon.[12] Every shop in Haworth closed on the day of Patrick's funeral, 12 June 1861, and every pew in the church was filled while hundreds of people stood outside in the churchyard. Many, we are told, shed tears. If those church building stones could have spoken!

Would they not have talked of William Grimshaw and John and Charles Wesley? Would they not have recalled the amazing scenes under George Whitfield in that very church as he preached from the scaffolding? Would they have poured out the tales of ferocious church rows around the appointment of Patrick Brontë forty-one years before? What would they have said of Mrs Maria Brontë and her children: Emily, Maria, Branwell, Elizabeth, Anne, and Charlotte?

The vicar of Bradford, Dr Burnett, and the Rev William Cartman jointly conducted Patrick's funeral service.[13] As Patrick's body was placed in the family vault, would the stones have told us of the day of his birth reckoned to be in the white-washed cabin of Hugh and Eleanor Brunty in the parish of Drumballyroney in Co Down in Ireland? 'The sting of death is sin, and the strength of sin is the law. But thanks be to God, which giveth us the victory through our Lord Jesus Christ,' wrote Paul in his great chapter on the nature of resurrection; this verse had been put on the memorial tablet to the Brontës in the church and Patrick's name was added.[14]

The following verse in Paul's summing-up of his great teaching regarding the resurrection urges the believer to the life of faith. There is no better epitaph for the life of Patrick Brontë: 'Therefore, my beloved brethren, be ye steadfast, unmovable, always abounding in the work of the Lord, forasmuch as ye know that your labour is not in vain in the Lord.' Patrick Brontë had put his hand to the Christian plough and, as far as his commitment to Christ was concerned, he did not look back. He was flawed, like all the rest of us, but he did abound in his Christian commitment and his labour was certainly not in vain. The fire of faith in his veins was never put out.

The trustees of Haworth church also proved to be as flawed in 1861 as the trustees with whom Patrick had dealt with in 1820. They rejected the Rev Arthur Nicholls as the next incumbent of Patrick's church. The vote was five to four against, with one abstention.[15] The *Bradford Observer* put it succinctly: 'The trustees will be asked by the country not whether their choice is a better man, but whether Mr Nicholls is unfit for the incumbency of Haworth? They are responsible, first to the parishioners, and next to all England for an answer. Have they interpreted the feelings of the parishioners correctly? Is it possible that the people of Haworth wished to turn adrift in a thankless manner a gentleman, no longer young, who had been for so many years their teacher in divine things?'[16]

Mr Nicholls took his disappointment with dignity and grace. Less than a month after the appointment of Patrick's successor, the Rev John Wade, Mr Nicholls left Haworth for Ireland.[17] He returned to Banagher with Patrick's dog, Plato, his wife's portrait, her wedding dress (of which a copy had been made), some of Charlotte's letters, other memorabilia and Martha Brown who wished to continue in his employment.[18] He never took up the Anglican ministry again and married his cousin, Mary Bell, nine-and-a-half years after Charlotte's death. Mary had travelled with Charlotte from Dublin to Banagher on her honeymoon and Charlotte had described her as the 'pretty lady-like girl with gentle English manners.'

Arthur died on 2 December 1906 at eighty-seven years of age, loved and respected by his community. He had deeply cherished his Brontë connections but had delighted in the peace and tranquillity of Banagher, far from the prying eyes of Brontë fans. When he died, Mary placed his coffin beneath a portrait of Charlotte, before it was removed for burial, showing her respect of Arthur's love for the great author.[19]

It was Ellen Nussey who took the full flow of interest in all things Brontë and she was consulted widely.[20] She was aghast at being criticised for supplying Mrs Gaskell with Charlotte's letters.[21] She particularly blamed Patrick and Arthur Nicholls for the censure she endured pointing out that they had insisted she lend the letters to Mrs Gaskell in the first place.[22] The truth is that if it had not been for Ellen's preservation of Charlotte's letters, we would never have known so much about the Brontë family.

Ellen was, in fact, the person asked to shut Charlotte's eyes when she had hastened to Haworth on hearing of her death.[23] She was, ultimately, the person who opened our eyes to the fire that ran in Brontë veins. Ellen Nussey died in November 1897 at eighty years of age and is buried in the cemetery of St Peter's Parish Church, Burstall. She certainly got pathetic praise for her contribution to the Brontë legacy while she lived, but she being dead, yet powerfully speaks. In terms of the Brontë legend, Ellen's dedication was beyond price.

By 1948, twenty-two million people are estimated to have seen *Wuthering Heights* and eighteen million to have seen *Jane Eyre* in motion picture.[24] Further films, television, opera, poetry and even song across recent decades have continued to make the novels of the Brontë sisters an indelible part of popular culture. Their voices continue to echo across the 21st century and the fire that ran in their veins still glows.

It is all, perhaps, best summed up in Jane Eyre's insistence that the fire should not be put out by marriage to St John Rivers: 'But as his wife – at his side always, and always restrained, and always checked – forced to keep the fire of my nature continually low, to compel it to burn inwardly and never utter a cry, though the imprisoned flame consumed vital after vital – *this* would be unendurable.'[25]

The fire in the Brontë veins and nature still inspires us as we turn to face a new century with all its challenges. If they could rise in their imaginations to such inspiring creativity from such oppression so, by the grace of God, can we.

One feels that a huge challenge particularly rises out of the Brontë story to 21st century writers, artists, film and documentary makers, playwrights and commentators who believe the Christian message. In an age where the Internet has changed our lives just as much as the Industrial Revolution changed the Yorkshire of the Brontë days, when travel is relatively cheap and worldwide, who is going to unashamedly dedicate their gift of creativity to the Lord Jesus and the spread of his gospel which is the best news in the world? Who, with fresh, inspiring language and a devoted heart is going to bring the moral values of the Bible to a world in dire need of them? One knows this will not be easy.

It is worthwhile listening again to Lucy Snowe in Charlotte Brontë's *Villette* turning to Imagination to inspire her in her loneliness. Dr John was writing letters to her and Lucy is thinking about the medium of writing. She is arguing with Reason: "'But,' I again broke in, "where the bodily presence is weak and the speech contemptible, surely there cannot be error in making written language the medium of better utterance than faltering lips can achieve?"

'Reason only answered, "At your peril you cherish that idea, or suffer its influence to animate any writing of yours!"

"But if I feel, may I *never* express?"

"*Never!*" declared Reason.

'I groaned under her bitter sternness. Never – never – oh, hard word! This hag, this Reason, would not let me look up, or smile, or hope: she could not rest unless I were altogether crushed, cowed, broken in and broken down. According to her, I was born only to work for a piece of bread, to await the pains of death, and steadily through all life to despond. Reason might be right; yet no wonder we are glad at times to defy her, to rush from under her rod and give a truant hour to Imagination – *her* soft, bright foe, *our* sweet Help, our divine Hope. We shall and must break bounds at intervals, despite the terrible revenge that awaits our return.

'Reason is vindictive as the devil; for me she was always envenomed as a stepmother. If I had obeyed her it has chiefly been with the obedience of fear, not of love. Long ago I should have died of her ill-usage: her stint, her chill, her barren board, her icy bed, her savage ceaseless blows; but for that kinder Power who holds my secret and sworn allegiance.

'Often has Reason turned me out by night, in mid-winter, on cold snow, flinging for sustenance the gnawed bone dogs had forsaken: sternly has she vowed her stores held nothing more for me – harshly denied my right to ask better things ... Then, looking up, have I seen in the sky a head amidst circling stars, of which the midmost and the brightest lent a ray sympathetic and attent.

'A spirit, softer and better than Human Reason, has descended with quiet flight to the waste – bringing all round her a sphere of air borrowed of eternal summer; bringing perfume of flowers which cannot fade – fragrance of trees whose fruit is life; bringing breezes pure from a world whose day needs no sun to lighten it. My hunger has this good angel appeased with food, sweet and strange, gathered amongst gleaning angels, garnering their dew-white harvest in the first fresh hour of a heavenly day; tenderly has she assuaged the insufferable fears which weep away life itself – kindly given rest to deadly weariness – generously lent hope and impulse to paralysed despair. Divine, compassionate, succourable influence!

'When I bend the knee to other than God, it shall be at thy white and winged feet, beautiful on mountain or on plain. Temples have been reared to the Sun – altars dedicated to the Moon. Oh, greater glory! To thee neither hands build, nor lips consecrate: but hearts, through ages, are faithful to thy worship. A dwelling thou hast, too wide for walls, too high for dome – a temple whose floors are space – rites whose mysteries transpire in presence, to the kindling, the harmony of worlds!

'Sovereign complete! thou hadst, for endurance, thy great army of martyrs; for achievement, thy chosen band of worthies. Deity unquestioned, thine essence foils decay! This daughter of Heaven remembered me tonight; she saw me weep, and she came with comfort: "Sleep," she said. "Sleep, sweetly – I gild thy dreams!"'

One can see in this passage that Lucy surely ranked Imagination highly and was plainly tempted to worship it. This would have been wrong. The next morning Reason returned and Lucy states: 'Sitting down before this dark comforter, I presently fell into a deep argument with myself on life and its chances, on destiny and her decrees. My mind, calmer and stronger now than last night, made for itself some imperious rules, prohibiting under deadly penalties all weak retrospect of happiness past; commanding a patient journeying through the wilderness of the present, enjoining a reliance on faith – a watching of the cloud and pillar which subdue while they guide, and awe while they illumine – hushing the impulse to fond idolatry, checking the longing outlook for a far-off promised land whose rivers are, *perhaps,*[26] ever to be reached save in dying dreams, whose sweet pastures are to be viewed but from the desolate and sepulchral summit of a Nebo.

'By degrees, a composite feeling of blended strength and pain wound itself wirily round my heart, sustained, or at least restrained, its throbbings, and made me fit for the day's work. I lifted my head.'[27]

One can see through this incredible piece of writing the tension Charlotte Brontë felt in her experience between the life of faith and the life of the imagination. It was a tension she had known since childhood. The use of the word *'perhaps'* is haunting. Lucy feels that she must stand like Moses on Mt Nebo firmly rooted in the life of faith but looking to the far-off promised land where, for her, the rivers of the life of imagination flow. She felt that *'perhaps'* those rivers could never be reached save in dying dreams.

In Charlotte Brontë's experience, the life of faith and the life of the imagination, one feels, are often set against each other. One wants to maintain that they do not need to be. Faith makes the imagination soar to places that can never be reached without it. A culture fed, for example, by drugs and alcohol and the worship of celebrity shows that its imagination produces bleakness, to say the least. The loss of true faith in any society is shown in the darkening of its imagination. Once faith is restored a renaissance of inspiration comes. This in turn, affects a culture's imagination in every corner.

Did not, for example, John Bunyan combine faith and imagination in his incredible *Pilgrim's Progress*, a copy of which stood in the Brontë library as the Brontë children grew up? Untold millions have been inspired by the way Bunyan used the medium of a dream to exquisitely expound the Christian pathway.

In the world of art, did not Holman Hunt combine his imagination and his faith in matchless paintings like *The Scapegoat*, *The Hireling*, *Conscience* and *The Light of the World*? Was not the evangelist Vincent van Gogh hassled by Christians to distraction so that he turned away from his evangelical work (though he never denied Christ) to exclusively painting when in truth, if he had only known it, he could have peacefully combined both? Who created a starry night and a sunflower in the first place?

From John Donne to C S Lewis, from George Herbert to Harriet Beecher Stowe, from John Milton to Harper Lee, from John Wycliffe to Eugene Peterson, from Augustine to Amy Carmichael, the list of Christians whose work has staggeringly combined imagination and faith stretches across the centuries since the dawn of Christianity.

One wants to declare that minds that have taken their thoughts and made them gloriously captivated by obedience to Christ[27] will find that imagination and faith can be combined to creatively inspire people anywhere. As Paul showed to the worshippers of the unknown God in Athens[28] – God can be known through faith in Jesus Christ. When he touches our imaginations, things of beauty emerge that can inspire us to leave this world a better place than we found it.   This combination, unquestionably, makes the purest fire in our veins.

Abbreviations

AB   Anne Brontë

AG   *Agnes Grey* (Penguin Popular Classics, London, 1994)

BP   Branwell Brontë

CB   Charlotte Brontë

EB   Emily Brontë

EG   Elizabeth Gaskell, *The Life of Charlotte Brontë* (Dent: London, Melbourne and Toronto, Everyman's Library, 1982)

JB   Juliet R V Barker, *The Brontës* (Weidenfeld and Nicolson, London, 1994)

JE   *Jane Eyre* (Penguin Classics, London, 2006)

L&D   John Lock and Canon W T Dixon, *A Man of Sorrow: The Life, Letters and Times of the Rev Patrick Brontë* (London, Nelson & Sons, 1965)

L&L   T J Wise and J A Symington, *The Lives, Friendships and Correspondence of the Brontë Family* (Oxford, Basil Blackwell, Shakespeare Head Press, 1934) 2 Vols.

PB   Patrick Brontë

S   Clement K Shorter, *Charlotte Brontë and Her Circle* (Hodder and Stoughton, 27 Paternoster Road, London, 1896)

WH   *Wuthering Heights* (Penguin Red Classic, 2006)

Notes

NOTES TO INTRODUCTION

1   CB to 'KT', 21 November 1850 (L&L, lll, 181).
2   Derick Bingham, *The Hawthorn Scent* (Ambassador International, 2000), p. 144.
3   See Michael Smith, *Last Man Standing?* (The Collins Press, Cork, 2006).
4   C S Lewis, *Surprised by Joy* (Inspirational Press, New York, 1991), p. 86.
5   Prof Sir Bernard Crossland, *The Lives of Great Engineers of Ulster* (NE Consultancy for Belfast Industrial Heritage), p. 64.
6   John Evangelist Walsh, *Darkling I Listen; The Last Days and Death of John Keats* (St Martin's Press, New York, 1999), p. 96.
7   *Ibid,* p. 97.
8   Joseph Severn, *On the Vicissitudes of Keat's Fame,* (Atlantic Monthly, April 1963, pp. 401-7).
9   Source, Seiyaku.com.
10 William Wright, *The Brontës in Ireland,* (Hodder & Stoughton, 1893), p. 249.
11 *Ibid,* p. 219. See photograph of cottage on frontispiece. There is no documentary evidence to support the identification.
12 Daily Telegraph, *Television and Radio,* 23-29 September 2006.
13 Lucasta Miller, *The Brontë Myth,* (Vintage, London, 2002), p. 175.
14 See Marianne Thormählen, *The Brontës and Religion,* (Cambridge University Press, Cambridge, 2004), pp. 54-5.
15 EB, WH, pp. 389-390.
16 EB, WH, p. 48.
17 EB, WH, p. 138.
18 CB, JE, p. 221.
19 Matthew Arnold, *Haworth Churchyard,* (Frasers Magazine, May 1855).
20 Lucasta Miller, *The Brontë Myth,* (Vintage, London, 2002), pp. 195-9.
21 AB, AG, pp. 10-11.

NOTES TO CHAPTER 1

1   C McCoy, Jack, *Ulster's Joan of Arc: An Examination of the Betsy Gray Story,* Bangor, 1989.
2   This poem and facts regarding the Battle of Ballynahinch are taken from *The Summer Soldiers: The 1798 Rebellion in Antrim and Down* by A T Q Stewart, (The Blackstaff Press, 1996).
3   Brontëana, p. 286.
4   EG, p. 21.
5   See JB, p. 3.

6   J A Venn, Alumni Cantabrigiensis (1752-1900) (Cambridge, CVP, 1951) Pt ii, pp. 189-190.
7   See JB, p. 4.
8   William Wordsworth, *The Prelude*, Book Xl (Oxford University Press, 1964), p. 570.
9   Alister McGrath, *The Twilight of Atheism: The Rise and Fall of Disbelief in the Modern World* (Rider, London, 2004), p. 21, pp. 29-30, p. 47.
10 John Wesley, *The Journal of John Wesley*, (24 May 1738) Christian Classics. Ethereal Library, online, in public domain. Print Basis. Moody Press, Chicago, 1951.
11 G O Trevelyan, *The Early History of Charles James Fox*, (1894), p. 83.
12 Francis Jeffrey, *Essays* (1853), p. 656.
13 *The Letters and Works of Lady Mary Worthy Montague*, Ed. W. Moy Thomas (1861), Vol. 1, p. 351. To The Countess of Marr, 31 October 1723.
14 A Skevington Wood, *The Burning Heart*, (The Paternoster Press), p. 9.
14 Alister McGrath, *The Twilight of Atheism: The Rise and Fall of Disbelief in the Modern World* (Rider, London, 2004), pp. 17-18.
16 Source S J Rogan, *John Wesley in Ireland*, 1747-1789, Vol. 2., Description on Mellon Press Website.
17 John Lock and Canon W T Dixon, *A Man of Sorrow: The Life, Letters and Times of the Rev Patrick Brontë* (London, Nelson & Sons, 1965), p. 11.
18 Marianne Thormahlen, *The Brontës and Religion* (Cambridge University Press, Cambridge 2004), pp. 13-14.
19 JB, p. 5.
20 William Wright, *The Brontës in Ireland*, (Hodder & Stoughton, 1893), p. 159-160.
21 EG, p. 22.

NOTES TO CHAPTER 2

1   *Henry Martyn to William Wilberforce,* February 1804 (L & D) p. 18.
2   Admissions Register 1802-35: MS C4.5 no. 1235, St John's College.
3   Residents Register: MS C27.1 no. 2, St John's College; see also JB, pp. 1-2 and Phyllis Bentley, *The Brontës and Their World* (Thames & Hudson, London, 1972), pp. 8-9.
4   *Ibid*, p. 9.
5   JB, p. 9.
6   Cambridge University Calendars (1804) p. 109; (1805), p. 190; (1806), p. 216.
7   *Henry Martyn to John Sargent*, c. Jan-Feb. 1804; MS Wilberforce, d. 14. p. 16 Bodleian.
8   Robin Furneaux, *William Wilberforce*, (London: Hamish Hamilton, 1974), pp. 118-119.
9   C *Henry Martyn to William Wilberforce*, 14 February 1804: MS. Wilberforce d. 14, p. 17, Bodelian (LND, p. 18).
10 *Ibid.*
11 L&L, ii, 212, 246.
12 Facts and quotations taken from Handley C G Moule, *Charles Simeon* (The Inter-Varsity Fellowship, London, 1952). First published 1892.
13 JB, p. 8.

14 *Cambridge Chronicle*, 2 June 1804, p. 4. EG, p. 22.

15 LND, p. 23.

16 William Wright, *The Brontës in Ireland*, (Hodder & Stoughton, 1893), p. 267.

NOTES TO CHAPTER 3

1   H M Dixon, *Reminiscences of an Essex County Practitioner a Century Ago*, The Essex Review, X1V (1915), p. 6.

2   Facts sourced in Augustine Birrell, *Life of Charlotte Brontë*, p. 20. L&L, I 68.

3   L&L, I 62.

4   Edmund Shorter, *The Brontës: Life and Letters,* I, 25 n. 2.

5   See argument in JB 20-23.

6   L&L, l 64.

7   Registers of Baptisms and Burials and of Marriages, All Saints Church, Wellington: MSS at All Saints, Wellington.

8   JB, p. 28.

9   A E Housman: *A Shropshire Lad ii: Loveliest of Trees, the Cherry Now.*

10 James Wood's Common Place Book, 1808-36, 6 November 1809. MS, M1-3, p. 214. St John's College.

11 Source: Frederick W Smith, 'Notes Towards a History of Dewsbury'(unpublished typescript, 1967): Local Studies Library, Castlegates, Dewsbury; Anon, *Memoir of the Rev John Buckworth.*

12 Yates, *The Father of the Brontës*, pp. 31-34.

13 JB, p. 38.

14 PB, *Sermon on the Epistle of Paul to the Romans 2:28-29* (c. 1811); MSBS 150. Pp. 2-3, 8, 19. Brontë Parsonage Museum, Haworth, West Yorkshire.

15 Luddites were a social movement of English Textile artisans in the 19th century who protested – often by destroying textile machines – against the changes produced by the industrial revolution which they felt threatened their livelihood. The original Luddites claimed to be led by a man called Ned Lunn.

16 C Kipling and Hall, on the Trial of the Luddites, p. 3, p. 9, pp. 31-36, 38-42, p. 49 and *Leeds Mercury* 18 April 1812, p. 3.

17 JB, p. 48.

18 L&N, I, 22-3.

19 Register of Marriages 1803-12, Guiseley Parish Church: MS p. 122, West Yorkshire Archive Service.

20 PB, *The Rural Minstrel*, pp. 47-8. (Brontiana, p. 83).

21 Register of Baptisms, St Peter's Church, Hartshead: Microfiche D 31/4 West Yorkshire Archive Service, Kirklees.

NOTES TO CHAPTER 4

1   Firth, Elizabeth, entries in her diaries made between 1812 and 1825. MS 589 A (MS Q 0 91 F), Firth Papers, University of Sheffield.

2   *The Pastoral Visitor*, July 1815, pp. 52-53.

3   Patrick Brontë, *The Cottage in the Wood*, or *The Art of Becoming Rich and Happy* (Bradford), T Inkersley, 1815), p. 5.

4   JB, p. 69.
5   L&L, l, 24.
6   PB, *The Maid of Killarney*, (London, Baldwin, Craddock & Joy, 1818).
7   *Ibid*, pp. 49-50.
8   JB, pp. 80-84; EG, pp. 18-20.
9   *The Leeds Intelligencer*, 22 November 1819, p. 2.
10 Joyce Eagleton, 5 April 1820; *The Story Tellers* (Bradford Libraries and Information Services 1990), p. 1.
11 See Fred Perry, *William Grimshaw: The Man Who Saw God Visit Howarth*, (Day One Publications, 2004).
12 EG, 14-16.
13 JB, p. 92.
14 Baines, *History, Directory and Gazetteer of the County of York*, (1822), I, 519.
15 Babbage: Report to the General Board of Health.
16 Baines, *History, Director and Gazetteer of the County of York* (1821), l, 519.
17 Charles Hale, *An American Visitor to Howarth*, 1861, Brontë Society, *Transactions* (Howarth 1895 to date); 5:77:134.
18 Firth (as in note one), 2nd, 4 January 1821.
19 L&L, l 58-60.
20 Register of Burials, 1813-36, Howarth Church.
21 L&L, I, 58-60.
22 L&L, l, 59.
23 J A V Chapple and Arthur Pollard (EDS), *The Letters of Mrs Gaskell* (Manchester, NVP, 1966), p. 124.
24 L&L, I, 59.
25 L A Herbert, *Charlotte Brontë: Pleasant Interview with the Old French Governess of this Famous Author.* Special correspondence of *The Post*, No. 7.
26 Register of Burials, 1813-36, Howarth Church.
27 L&L, I, 59.

NOTES TO CHAPTER 5

1   See background to this assertion, JB note 70, p. 854.
2   *Ibid*, note 71 p. 855.
3   EG, pp. 29-30.
4   (Nancy Garrs) *Illustrated Weekly Telegraph*, 10 January 1885, p. 1.
5   William Dearden to *Bradford Observer* 20 August 1857, p. 8.
6   Sarah Garrs, quoted in Harland, *Charlotte Brontë at Home*, p. 32.
7   Isabella Drury to Miss Mariner, 14 February, 1823; MS Bl lX DF p. 1, Brontë Parsonage Museum.
8   L&L, 1, 61.
9   L&L, 1, 62-63.
10 L&L, 1, 65-66.
11 L&L, 1, 67.
12 *Leeds Intelligencer* December 1823, p. 1.
13 Admissions Register, No. 30.
14 L&L, ii, 150.
15 *Ibid*.
16 EG, pp. 43-44.

17   EG, p. 44.
18   JB, p. 125, also note 42, p. 857.
19   EG, p. 45.
20   EG, p. 48.
21   The Register of Burials, 1813-36, Haworth Church.
22   Mrs Ellis H Chadwick, *In the Footsteps of the Brontës*, (London, Pitman & Sons, 1914), p. 78.
23   Ledger of the Clergy Daughters' School, 31 May 1825; MSWD 5/338/1, p. 13, Cumbria Record Office, Kendal.
24   Note 22, p. 78; Admissions Register, Nos. 30-44.
25   JB, pp. 145-147.
26   Gordon Bottomley, *Memoirs of Alfred Bottomley* (reprinted from New Church Magazine for January 1932), p. 8. Keighley.
27   JB, p. 150.
28   *Leeds Intelligencer,* 15 January, p. 4; 29 June, pp. 4-5; 5 February, p. 4, 1829.
29   *Leeds Mercury,* 10 January 1829, p. 4.
30   L&L, I, 186.

NOTES TO CHAPTER 6

1   Joan Stevens (ed.) Mary Taylor, *Friend of Charlotte Brontë: Letters from New Zealand and Elsewhere* (Oxford OUP, 1972).
2   Phyllis Bentley, *The Brontës and their World*, (Thames and Hudson, London, 1972), p. 41.
3   Ellen Nussey, *Reminiscences,* Brontë Society *Transactions,* (Howarth, 1895 to date): 2: 10: 59-60.
4   JB, p. 172.
5   Joan Stevens (see note 1), pp.158-9.
6   Stevens (see note 1), p. 163.
7   Ellen Nussey, (see note 3): 2, 10: 64-5.
8   *Ibid,* p. 63.
9   C K Shouter, p. 205.
10   Ellen Nussey, (see note 3), pp. 52-56.
11   JB, p. 195.
12   JB, p. 201.
13   M S Ashley, *Manuscript Collection, British Library,* London.
14   EG, p. 87.
15   EG, p. 88.
16   L&L, 1, 209.
17   T J Wise and J A Symington (eds.), *The Miscellaneous and Unpublished Writings of Charlotte Brontë and Patrick Branwell Brontë* (Oxford, Basil Blackwell, Shakespeare Head Press, 1934), ii, 123-4.
18   See note 2, p. 50.
19   EG, p. 93.
20   See note 2, p. 50.
21   *Ibid*, pp. 50-51.
22   EG, p. 94.

23 L&L, 1, 155.
24 L&L, 1, 157-8.
25 L&L, 1, 147.
26 See note 3; 1: 7: 27.
27 William Wilberforce, *A Practical View of the Prevailing Religious System* (Glasgow editon,1838), p. 44.
28 Count Nikolaus Ludwig von Zinzendorf (1700-60).
29 James de la Trobe to William Scruton, n.d: quoted in William Scruton, 'Reminiscences of the late Miss Ellen Nussey, Brontë Society *Transactions* (Howarth, 1895 to date):1:7:27.

NOTES ON CHAPTER 7

1 Emily Jane Brontë: *'Loud Without the Wind was roaring'* 11 November 1838: MS. In Law Collection (facsimile in *Poems of EJB and AB,* p. 302; Hatfield, p. 92*).*
2 L&L 1, 167-8.
3 CB, *'All this Day I have been in a dream'* 11 August-14 October 1836: MS. Bon 98 (8), pp. 1-2, Brontë Parsonage Museum.
4 L&L, 1, 166.
5 CB, *'A Young Gentleman of Captivating Exterior'* (Henry Hastings), 24 February-26 March 1839: MS. in Widener Collection, Harvard, pp. 256-7.
6 L&L, 1, 172.
7 *Ibid.*
8 Anne Brontë, *Agnes Grey* (Penguin Popular Classics, London, 1994), pp. 63-65.
9 Susan Brook, *Anne Brontë at Blake Hall*, Brontë Society, *Transactions* (Haworth, 1845 to date): 13: 68: 247.
10 CB, *Biographical Notice of Ellis and Acton Bell,* 19 September 1850, Source, see note 8.
11 See note 8, p. 301.
12 CB, *Biographical Notice of Ellis and Acton Bell,* 19 September 1850.
13 EG, p. 114.
14 Victor Neufeldt (ed.), *The Poems of Patrick Branwell Brontë, A New Text and Commentary,* (New York, Garland Publishing, 1985), pp. 202-9. Patrick Branwell Brontë to Hartley Coleridge, 20 April 1840: MS in Law Collection, transcript in Ratchford Papers, Texas. (Poem was entitled, 'At dead of midnight-drearily').
15 *Ibid,* p. 443.
16 L&L, 1, 210.
17 Lord Houghton, MS. *Common Place Book,* 1857-60, p. 338, The Library, Trinity College, Cambridge.
18 *Halifax Guardian,* 18 April 1846, p. 6.
19 EG, p. 139.
20 CB *Villette,* Ch. 6., online-literature.com, The Literature Network.
21 William Wordsworth, *Composed upon Westminster Bridge,* 2 September 1802 (Penguin Classics, London, 2004), pp. 150-151.
22 Benjamin Binns, *Bradford Observer,* 17 February 1894, p. 6.
23 Richard Holmes, *Wellington*: *The Iron Duke* (Harper Collins Publishers, London, 2002), p. 227.

24 *Ibid*, p. 228.
25 Wellesley, op. cit, p. 367.
26 Note 23, p. 250.
27 Weller, *Waterloo*, op. cit, p. 154.
28 Shelley I, p. 102.
29 See note 22.
30 JB, p. 364.
31 Emily Brontë, *Wuthering Heights*, (Penguin Books, London, Red Classic, 2006), p. 94.
32 2 Peter 3:10.
33 Romans 8:18-25. Scripture taken from The Holy Bible, New International Version. NIV. Copyright 1973, 1978, 1984, by International Bible Society. Used by permission of Zondervan Publishing House. All rights reserved.

NOTES ON CHAPTER 8

1 L&L, 1, 266-7.
2 EG, p. 150
3 Source Macdonald, *The Brontës at Brussels*, *The Women at Home*, pp. 283-4.
4 Constantin Heger, *Conseil*, at the end of CB. 'Le Nid' 30 April 1842: MS. p. 4. Berg (translation Brontë Society *Transactions* (Haworth,1845 to date) 6: 83: 213-14.
5 Funeral Sermon ... for William Weightman, pp. 12-13 (Brontëana, p. 259).
6 Elizabeth Branwell, Probate Papers, 21 November-28 December 1842; MS Probate, Borthwick.
7 CB, *Villette,* ch. XV online-literature.com, The Literature Network.
8 EG, p. 168.
9 Lenoff, C B *Belgium Essays: The Discourse of Empowerment,* pp. 287-409.
10 JB, p. 417. See also her discussion of the Nature of Genius between CB and C Heger, pp. 414-417.
11 JB, p. 419.
12 EG, p. 177.
13 See Dr Tess O'Toole, *Introduction to CB, Complete and Unabridged* (Barnes and Noble, New York, 2006), p. 1X.
14 CB, *Villette,* ch. XV, online-literature.com, The Literature Network.
15 EG, p. 177.
16 L&L, 1, 305-6.
17 Patricia Ingham, *The Brontës* (Oxford University Press, Oxford, 2006) p. 188.
18 *Ibid*, p. 188. Quoted from CB, *The Professor*, chapter 12.
19 CB, *Villette,* ch. XV, online-literature.com, The Literature Network.
20 See Note 17, p. 190.
21 JB, p. 424.
22 See note 16, p. 304.
23 L&L, 1, 306-7.
24 *Ibid.*
25 *Halifax Guardian*, 29 July 1843, p. 3.
26 L&D, 334-5.
27 *Leeds Mercury*, 15 July 1843, p. 6.
28 *Leeds Intelligencer*, 2 September 1843, p. 8.

29 John Pollock, *Wilberforce* (Lion Publishing), Berkhamstead, 1978, p. 162.
30 *Bradford Observer*, 28 December 1843, p. 5.
31 *Leeds Mercury*, 16 March 1834, p. 6.
32 Marianne Thormahlen, *The Brontës and Religion*, (Cambridge University Press, Cambridge, 2004), p. 88.
33 Romans 3:22-24.
34 Quoted in Phyllis Bentley: *The Brontës and Their World*, (Thames and Hudson, London, 1972), p. 79.
35 *Ibid*, p. 80.
36 Currer, Ellis and Acton Bell, *Poems*, (Aylott and Jones, 1846), pp. 60-75.
37 L&L, 2, 28.
38 L&L, 2, 43.
39 *Ibid.*
40 Phyllis Bentley: *The Brontës and their World* (Thames and Hudson, London,1972), p. 85.
41 *Halifax Guardian,* 8 November 1845, p. 6 and 20 December 1845, p. 6.
42 L&L, ii, 60.

NOTES TO CHAPTER 9

1 CB, *Biographical Notice of Ellis and Acton Bell*, 19 September 1850, *Agnes Grey* (Penguin Popular Classics, London, 1994), pp. 2-4.
2 Phyllis Bentley, *The Brontës and Their World* (Thames and Hudson, London, 1972), p. 87.
3 EG, p. 207.
4 JB, pp. 497-8.
5 EG, p. 215.
6 EG, p. 209.
7 L&L, ll, 109.
8 L&L, ll, 108-9.
9 CB, *Jane Eyre* (Penguin Classics, London, 2006), p. 9.
10 Harriet Martineau, Obituary of CB in the *Daily News*, 6 April 1855 (Allott, p. 303).
11 A N Wilson, *Daily Telegraph,* 30 April 2007.
12 Proverbs 14:34.
13 CB, *Jane Eyre*, (Penguin Classics, London, 2006), p. 365.
14 *Ibid*, p. 467.
15 *Ibid*, p. 467.
16 *Ibid*, p. 405.
17 *Ibid*, p. 517.
18 *Ibid*, p. 516.
19 Harriet Martineau, Obituary of CB in the *Daily News*, 6 April 1855 (Allott, pp. 303-4).
20 JB, pp. 512-514.
21 L&L, 2, 117-18.
22 EG, p. 196.
23 L&L, ll, 117.
24 *Leeds Intelligencer,* 27 March 1847, p. 6.
25 *Leeds Mercury*, 5 June 1847, p. 7.

26 *Leeds Intelligencer*, 25 September 1847, p. 6.
27 Manuscript Brontë Society x, H, The Library, Brontë Parsonage Museum, Haworth, Yorkshire.
28 *Halifax Guardian,* 5 June 1847, p. 6.
29 L&L, lll, 156.
30 L&L, lll, 139.
31 CB, *Biographical Notice,* p. 361.
32 EG, p. 224.
33 EG, pp. 215-216.
34 Based on George Smith, *A Memoir*, with some pages of Autobiography (London, Private Circulation, 1902) pp. 87-88.
35 CB, to Smith, Elder & Company, 12 September 1847: Manuscript S-G IP p.2., Brontë Parsonage Museum.
36 *Ibid,* pp. 1-2.
37 EG, p. 230.
38 W M Thackeray to W S Williams, 23 October 1847. Ray, *The Letters and Private Papers of William Makepeace Thackeray*, ll, 318-19.
39 CB, Preface to *Jane Eyre,* 21 December 1847 (Penguin Classics, London, 2006), pp. 5-6.
40 Phyllis Bentley, *The Brontës and Their World* (Thames and Hudson, London, 1972), p. 91.
41 See William Wright, *The Brontës in Ireland,* (Hodder & Stoughton, London, 1893).
42 Emily Brontë, *Wuthering Heights* (Penguin Red Classic, 2000), p. 4.
43 *Ibid,* p. 200.
44 *Ibid,* pp. 357-358.
45 *Ibid,* p. 359.
46 *Ibid,* p. 138.
47 AB, *The Tenant of Wildfell Hall,* Preface to the Second Edition, 22 July 1848, (Penguin Popular Classics, 1994) p. 18.
48 Lucasta Millar, *The Brontë Myth* (Vintage, London, 2002) pp. 156-7. AB, *The Tenant of Wildfell Hall,* (Penguin Popular Classics, London, 1994), p. 14.
49 Phillippa Stone, *The Captive Dove,* (London, 1959).
50 L&L, l, 219.
51 Based on L&L, ll, 130-1.
52 See note one, pp. 8-9.
53 *Ibid,* p. 8.
54 Lucasta Miller, *The Brontë Myth,* (Vintage, London, 2002) pp. 156-157.
55 See note 47, pp. 18-19.
56 L&L, ll, p. 148.
57 L&L, ll, p. 178.
58 L&L, ll, p. 178
59 L&L, ll, p. 226. EG, p. 247.
60 Joan Stevens (ed), (*Mary Taylor: Friend of Charlotte Brontë: letters from New Zealand and Elsewhere* (Oxford, OUP, 1972) p. 178.
61 EG, p. 248.
62 EG, p. 252.
63 EG, pp. 249-252.
64 L&L, ll, p. 230.
65 L&L, ll, p. 165.

NOTES TO CHAPTER 10

1   EG, p. 255.
2   EG, pp. 197-198.
3   See Francis H Grundy, *Picture of the Past* (London, Griffith & Farrer, 1879), pp. 90-92.
4   L&L, 211, 262-3; Leyland, ll, 278-9.
5   CB to W S Williams, 6 October 1848, Clement Shorter, *Charlotte Brontë and Her Circle* (Hodder & Stoughton, London, 1896), p. 140.
6   CB to W S Williams, 2 October 1848, Clement Shorter, *Charlotte Brontë and Her Circle*, p. 188 (Hodder & Stoughton, London, 1896), p. 138.
7   *Ibid*, p. 139.
8   Register of Burials, 1836-54, Haworth Church: no. 1756 (28 September 1848).
9   EG, p. 255.
10 EG, p. 256.
11 L&L, ll, 184.
12 L&L, ll, 117.
13 L&L, ll, 184.
14 Believed to have been written by John Lockhart and John Wilson, *Blackwood's Magazine*, August 1818.
15 Thomas Carlyle, Review of Moncton Milne's, *Life of Keats*.
16 CB, *Biographical Notice of Ellis & Acton Bell*, 19 September 1850 (Penguin Popular Classics, London, 1994), pp. 9-10.
17 EG, pp. 257-8.
18 *Ibid*, p. 258.
19 *Ibid*, p. 259.
20 Ellen Nussey, *Reminiscences,* Brontë Society, *Transactions* (Haworth 1895 to date): 8: 42: 21.
21 AB, *Music on Christmas Morning*, from *Poems* by Currer & Acton Bell (Alyott & Jones, 8 Paternoster Row, 1846), pp. 45-46.
22 AB, *A dreadful darkness closes in*,7-28 January 1849: MS Bon 137 pp. 1-2, Brontë Parsonage Museum. See JB, p. 582 and p. 942, note 47.
23 EG, p. 267.
24 L&L, ll, 312-313.
25 L&L, ll, 37.
26 L&L, ll, 318.
27 L&L, ll, 325.
28 EG, p. 271.
29 Information taken from Tourist Information UK online.
30 EG, p. 271.
31 L&L, ll, 330.
32 Ellen Nussey, *A Short Account of the Last Days of Dear Anne Brontë*: MS, pp. 4-7, Hugh Walpole Collection, The Library, Kings School, Canterbury, Kent: EG, p. 271.
33 EG, p. 272.
34 Ellen Nussey, *Reminiscences,* R. p. 96.
35 EG, pp. 272-3.
36 L&L, ll, p. 339.
37 EG, p. 273.
38 EG, p. 274.
39 L&L, lll, p. 336.
40 EG, pp. 374-375.
41 EG, p. 375.

NOTES TO CHAPTER 11

1   EG, p. 278.
2   *Ibid.*
3   EG, p. 277.
4   *Shirley*, chapter 24, online-literature.com, The Literature Network.
5   *Ibid,* chapter 25.
6   CB, *A Word to the 'Quarterly'*, 29 August 1849, MS S-G 96 p. 1, Brontë Parsonage Museum.
7   EG, pp. 279-280.
8   JB, p. 609; L&L, ll, 303.
9   David Harrison, *The Brontës of Haworth*; Yorkshire's Literary Giants (Trafford, Victoria, BC, Canada), p. 90.
10 S, pp. 347-8.
11 L&L, ll, 313.
12 Charles Kingsley to EG, 14 May 1857(Miriam Allott (ed.), *The Brontës: The Critical Heritage* (London, Routledge & Kegan Paul, 1974).
13 CB, *Shirley*, chapter 37, online-literature.com, The Literature Network.
14 L&L, lll, 71.
15 CB, *Shirley*, chapter 22, online-literature.com, The Literature Network.
16 EG, p. 277.
17 L&L, lll, 34.
18 Brontë Society, *Transactions* (Howarth, 1895 to date), 18: 92: 104; 18: 92: 104-5; 18: 95: 105-6.
19 CB to Margaret Wooller, 14 February,1850, MS FM 8, pp. 6-7, Department of Manuscripts, Fitzwilliam Museum, Cambridge.
20 W M Thackeray, *The Last Sketch*, Cornhill, 1 Jan-June 1860, p. 486.
21 Harriett Martineau, *Autobiography*, pp. 323-5.
22 EG, pp. 287-9.
23 Deuteronomy 23:35 (King James Version).
24 *Leeds Intelligencer,* 22 December 1849, p. 7.
25 Luke 9:62 (King James Version).
26 L&L, lll, p.63.
27 L&L, lll, p.73.
28 *Bradford Observer,* 28 February 1850, p. 5.
29 EG, pp. 295-6.
30 EG, p. 297.
31 L&L, lll, 107.
32 Babbage Report, pp. 12, 26-7.
33 EG, p. 304; S, pp. 450-451; L&L lll, p. 117; George Smith, *A Memoir with some pages of Autobiography* (London, Private Circulation, 1902) p. 92.
34 Thackeray Ritchie ,*Chapters from Some Memoirs.*
35 George Smith, *A Memoir with some pages of Autobiography,* (London, Private Circulation, 1902) p. 98.
36 See note 34.
37 EG, pp. 307-8.
38 See Note 35, p. 104.
39 Sidney Lee, *Charlotte Brontë in London,* Brontë Society *Transactions* (Howarth, 1895 to date), 14: 19: 116.
40 S, pp. 452-3.

41 Phyllis Bentley, *The Brontës and Their World,* (Thomas & Hudson, London), pp. 110-11.
42 EG, p. 306.

NOTES TO CHAPTER 12

1   L&L, lll, p. 139.
2   EG, pp. 309-10.
3   L&L, lll, p. 60.
4   EG, p. 323.
5   *Leeds Intelligencer*, 19 October 1850, p. 6.
6   L&L, lll, p. 199.
7   Arnold, *The Poems,* p. 401.
8   Arnold, *Literature & Dogma*, p. 145.
9   *Poems* by Currer, Ellis & Acton Bell, (Alyott & Jones, 8 Paternoster Row, 1846), pp. 1-7. See also Matthew 27:19.
10 EG, p. 329.
11 See Derick Bingham, *The Love Unknown* (available from www.tbft.tv and published by the TBF and K L Thompson Trust).
12 EG, p. 331.
13 L&D, p. 436.
14 L&L, lll, p. 239.
15 EG, pp. 337-8.
16 EG, p. 335.
17 L&L, lll, pp. 248-9.
18 EG, pp. 336-7.
19 EG, p. 345.
20 L&L, lll, pp. 306-7, 285.
21 JB, p. 695.
22 EG, pp. 359-60.
23 L&L, lV, p. 13.
24 EG, p. 365.
25 L&L, lV, p. 20.
26 EG, p. 369.
27 EG, p. 371.
28 L&L, lV, pp. 29-30.
29 S, p. 475.
30 S, p. 476.
31 EG, p. 372.
32 EG, p. 373.
33 L&L, lV, p. 40.
34 EG, p. 374.
35 Harriet Martineau, Review in the *Daily News*, 3 February 1853, pp. 128-9.
36 L&L, lV, pp. 49-50.
37 JB, pp. 716-7, 725.
38 S, p. 478.
39 S, p. 479.
40 S, p. 479.
41 S, p. 480.

42 *Leeds Intelligencer*, 28 May 1853, p. 8.
43 S, p. 481.

NOTES TO CHAPTER 13

1   Brontë Society, *Transactions*, (Haworth, 1895 to date): 9: 46: 4-5.
2   L&L, lV, p. 71.
3   L&L, lV, p. 78.
4   *Christian Remembrancer*, April 1853. pp. 401-43. (Miriam Allott (ed.), *The Brontës: The Critical Heritage* (London, Routledge and Kegan Paul, 1974).
5   CB, To the Editor of the *Christian Remembrancer*, 18 July 1853: MS. n.l, (W Robertson Nicoll, *Charlotte Brontë and one of her Critics*, *The Bookman* , November 1899.
6   L&L, lV, p. 124.
7   L&L, lV, p. 101.
8   L&L, lV, pp. 81-2; L&L, lV, p. 101.
9   JB, p. 741.
10 Charlotte Brontë to Mrs Smith, 21 November 1853; MS S-G-86, p. 2 Brontë Parsonage Museum; Mrs Smith to Charlotte Brontë (see 22 November 1853): MS s-g 87 p. 1, Brontë Parsonage Museum.
11 Brontë Society, *Transactions,* (Haworth 1895 to date): 18: 92: 113.
12 L&L, lV, p. 112.
13 L&L, lV, p. 113.
14 L&L, lV, p. 101.
15 L&L, lV, p. 107.
16 L&L, lV, p. 112.
17 L&L, lV, pp. 112-13.
18 EG, p. 387.
19 L&L, lV, p. 16.
20 John Robinson, *Love Story of Charlotte Brontë: Wedding Recollected;* Keighley News, 27 October 1923, p. 8.
21 EG, p. 395; L&L, lV, p. 143.
22 *Jane Eyre* (Penguin Classics, London, 2006), p. 333.
23 *Ibid*, p. 368.
24 EG, p. 395.
25 See note 20; Ellen Nussey to George Smith, 28 March 1860, MS File 7 no 4, John Murray.
26 L&L, ll, p. 136.
27 EG, p. 395.
28 L&L, lV, p. 148.
29 L&L, lV, p. 136; L&L,1V,pp. 137-8.
30 L&L, lV, p. 143.
31 L&L, lV, p. 138.
32 EG, p. 396.
33 L&L, lV, p. 149.
34 L&L, lV, p. 157.
35 L&L, lV, p. 157.
36 JB, p. 767.

37 L&L, lV, p. 166; L&L, lV, pp. 163-4.
38 See Note 11: 16: 81: 19.
39 Phyllis Bentley, *The Brontës and Their World,* (Thames & Hudson, London, 1972), p. 120: L&L, lV, pp. 164-5.
40 L&L, lV, p. 171.
41 L&L, lV, p. 173.
42 EG, p. 400.
43 For an in-depth look at the cause of Charlotte's death, see JB, p. 967, note 96.
44 EG, p. 401.
45 Register of Burials,1854-84, Haworth Church.
46 Whitley Turner, *A Springtime Saunter Round and About Brontëland*, p. 199
47 EG, p. 401.

NOTES TO CHAPTER 14

1   Brontë Society, *Transactions* (Haworth, 1895 to date): 8: 44: 129.
2   JB, p. 791.
3   *The Times,* 30 May 1857, p. 5.
4   *The Leeds Intelligencer* and *Leeds Mercury,* 16 May 1857.
5   William Dearden to *Bradford Observer,* 13 May 1857, p. 7 and 20 August 1857, p. 8.
6   Harriet Martineau to *Daily News,* 24 August 1857,
7   *Bradford Observer,* 9 August 1860, p. 5.
8   *Ibid,* 16 August, p. 5.
9   *The Halifax Courier,* 16 February 1861, p. 5; 23 March 1861, p. 5.
10 Job 19:25-27 (King James Version).
11 Robert Browning, *Prospice,* Representative Poetry Online.
12 Arthur Nicholls to George Smith, 25 June 1861; MS File 8 no. 20 p. 2, John Murray.
13 *The Leeds Intelligencer,* 15 June 1861, p. 5; *Bradford Review,* 13 June 1861, p. 2; *Halifax Guardian,* 15 June 1861, p. 5.
14 1 Corinthians 15:56-58 (King James Version).
15 'N' to *Bradford Review,* 12 October 1861, p. 5.
16 *Bradford Observer,* 26 September 1861, p. 4.
17 Charles Hale to his mother, 11 November 1861 *(An American Visitor at Haworth 1861),* Brontë Society, *Transactions:* 15: 77: 128.
18 Phyllis Bentley, *The Brontës and Their World* (Thames & Hudson, London, 1972), p. 126.
19 Marjorie Gallop, *Charlotte's Husband: Sidelights from a Family Album,* Brontë Society, *Transactions* (Haworth 1895, to date); 12: 64: 298-9.
20 William Santon, *Reminiscences of the late Miss Ellen Nussey,* Brontë Society, *Transactions* (Haworth 1895, to date): 1: 7: 24-42.
21 JB, p. 828.
22 *Ibid,* p. 828.
23 *Ibid,* JB, p. 773.
24 Patricia Ingham, *Authors in Context, The Brontës,* (Oxford World Classics, 2006), p. 228.
25 Charlotte Brontë, *Jane Eyre,* (Penguin Classics, London, 2006), p. 470.

26 The author's emphasis.
27 Charlotte Brontë, *Villette*, chapter 21, online-literature.com, The Literature Network.
28 2 Corinthians 10:5.
29 Acts 17:23-32.